Mother's Table, Father's Chair

Cultural Narratives of
Basque American Women

Mother's Table, Father's Chair

Cultural Narratives of
Basque American Women

Jacqueline S. Thursby

Utah State University Press
Logan, Utah
1999

F
596.3
.B15
T48
1999

To Louise, Cecelia, Virginia, Isabel,
other Basque American women of the West,
their mothers, their daughters, and their granddaughters

Utah State University Press
Logan, Utah 84322-7800

Typography by WolfPack
Cover Design by Karen Groves

Library of Congress Cataloging-in-Publication Data

Thursby, Jacqueline S., 1940-
Mother's table, father's chair : cultural narratives of Basque
American women / Jacqueline S. Thursby.
p. cm.
ISBN 0-87421-265-0
ISBN 0-87421-264-2 (pbk.)
1. Basque American women—West (U.S.)—Social life and customs.
2. West (U.S.)—Social life and customs. I. Title.
F596.3.B15 T48 1999
305.4'089'9992078—dc21
98-58072
CIP

Contents

Acknowledgments

I wish to acknowledge those people who lent their support, guidance, and effort toward the successful completion of this project. Sincere appreciation is expressed to my colleague and mentor, Dr. William A. Wilson, professor emeritus, Brigham Young University, for guiding and encouraging me to continue the process of converting the dissertation to a monograph. I would like to thank my former advisors, Dr. Barre Toelken of Utah State University and Dr. William H. Grant of Bowling Green State University, for their constant direction and encouragement from the project's initial stages to its completion. I would like to thank Dr. John Alley, executive editor of Utah State University Press, for his patience and encouragement.

Sincere gratitude is also extended to the Basque American women who generously shared their stories for this collection.

Lastly, and most importantly, I want to acknowledge and express my sincere gratitude to my family. I extend the warmest appreciation to my husband, Denny; our children, Chris, Michelle, Valerie, and Will; and grandchildren, Amanda, Ben, Chad, Nick, Nolan, Sarah, Ellen, and Nathan. Their joyfulness and good will have served as an inspiration toward the accomplishment of this goal.

The bride is a flower;
She has a laugh on her lips,
The bridegroom who is betrothed this eve
Is her equal.[1]

Left to right: The author, Shirley Crystal (cook), and Louise Etcheverry in the cook house at the Etcheverry Ranch, Rupert, Idaho.

Basque American country: the Jouglard-Dredge Ranch, Caribou County, Idaho.

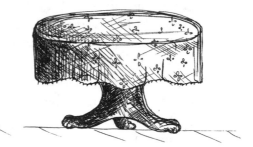

Introduction

Early one autumn morning a few years ago I was driving on a highway in Caribou County, Idaho, and unexpectedly came upon a huge band of sheep. I slowed down and realized that I would not be continuing my journey until the sheep were safely across the highway. I turned off the engine and prepared to watch something I had never seen before. Soon my car was surrounded by hundreds of wooly animals being driven along by sheepmen on horses assisted by energetic border collies. I faintly heard the men calling to one another, so I rolled down the car window and heard a buoyant, musical language entirely new to my ears. It wasn't French or Spanish. The cadence and the rhythm of the voices was unique and strangely musical, and I wanted to know more.

Later that morning at the high school where I taught, I inquired about what I had seen and heard on the way to school. I was told that the herders were Basques and not particularly friendly with outsiders. My acquaintances mentioned that the surnames of Basques and those of the Spanish and Mexicans living in the area differed somewhat in spelling and sound. I was curious, and not knowing quite what I was looking for, I soon visited the city hall to see if there were people with Basque sounding names living in Caribou County. There were several. I was told that all the Basques in the region were sheepherders. I hoped to meet some of them and learn about their culture, folklore, and occupations, so my next stop was at the office of the county agricultural agent, Ed Duren. He knew all of the Basque American families in the region and offered to introduce me, by telephone, to three of the women. At his desk in his well-worn office filled with stacks of mail, tall file cabinets, boxes of sheep and farm magazines, and hundreds of agricultural and animal husbandry books, Mr. Duren dialed the numbers and introduced me to three courteous Basque American women: Louise Savala Etcheverry, Alicia Aldana Dredge, and Resu Goldaraz Goldaraz.

Within a few weeks I had conducted my first tape-recorded interviews with each of them, and they in turn introduced me to other women. Their stories reflected a strong sense of community shaped by the folklore and traditions of cultures in both the old country and in the United States. They were eager to answer questions and share information because, they told me, their stories had not been gathered and time was passing quickly. They asked if I would write their accounts, and so, this text is a reciprocal writing effort between the women and me. I sent copies of what I wrote to them, and they made corrections and changes for clarification and accuracy. I have served "as scribe and archivist as well as [a cautious] interpreting observer" (Clifford and Marcus 1986, 17), though ultimately I have arranged the presentation of information.[2]

Folklorists have taught that traditional expressive behavior maintained by a particular ethnic community publicly and privately demarcates one ethnic individual or community from another (Danielson 1977, 1–5). That is true, but as this study will demonstrate, the Basques of the American West have realized that as Americans, a definition almost synonymous with diversity, the celebration of their unique ethnic heritage has a better chance of survival if they sometimes blend it, at least at the margins, with other ethnic groups.

It is significant that the women all mentioned that being Basque in America is a different experience than that of their relatives still living in the old country, and they were conscious also of cultural adaptations made by Basques in South America and Mexico where Spanish is the main language. They seemed to hold tightly to the concept that their common customs, kinship ties, and shared or collective memories bind all of the participants in the Basque diaspora together.

The cultural and personal narratives shared in the following pages have been shaped by gatekeepers—individuals who hope to keep a traditional and "created ethnicity" (Stern and Cicala 1991) safe from dissolution. Their invented narratives help keep the Basque American culture vibrant. "Invented narrative" does not imply a lack of veracity but rather the dynamic and conservative tension that Barre Toelken illuminated in his discussion of the "Twin Laws" of folklore (1996, 39, 43). "Balancing the dynamism of change in performance is the essentially conservative force of the tradition itself" (39), and that, essentially, is what many Basque American women do. They have mastered the articulation of their culture. They are practiced and skilled performers who, through their shaped and reshaped narratives, choose to create a context for the continuation of an invented Basque American ethnicity.

After interviewing the first three women, I conducted a search to learn how much information had been published about them in the United States. I was told by a male Basque referred to me that there was no point in developing a work about the Basque American women. He said: "What? The women? What have they done to contribute anything to this culture? The men have done it all!" His attitude represents a minority; most of the men I visited with acknowledged the powerful influences their mothers, wives, or daughters have had in their lives. And, having interviewed individuals from three generations in six Western states, and two generations in the old country, I have come to perceive these women as skilled cultural architects and guardians. They continually assess and, if necessary, redesign forms of their inherited cultural elements to ensure that those important markers function appropriately in a rapidly changing world society.

The women were correct in their assessment concerning what had been recorded about them. Very little of the women's part in shaping the Basque American culture has been collected and written. The Basque anthropologist Teresa del Valle, of the Basque Country in northern Spain, has researched and published extensively on the women of her homeland. There are a few master's theses on the topic of Basque American women and their traditions, and I found an excellent dissertation on the Basque hotels in America written in 1988 by Jerònima Echeverria. The informative dissertation included some discussion of women, but it was not based primarily on their own vernacular stories. I perused the Basque Studies Library at the University of Nevada-Reno, and found a large collection of books, videos, and tapes about the Basque Country and its history written for the most part in Basque, French, or Spanish. Immigration stories are being collected and studied at the Basque Museum in Boise, Idaho, and enthusiastic Basque American scholars, men and women, are emerging from the Basque Studies Program at the University of Nevada, Reno, with interests that range from folk dance to Basque literature to genetics. At the Basque Studies Library in Reno, Marcelino Ugalde, librarian, loaned me several articles about Basque women and gave me access to tape-recorded interviews housed there. Part of the following work is based on those valuable tapes and articles. Other than a few essays in American anthropological publications and brief mention in texts and cookbooks written about Basques in America, I found little additional recorded information about the women and their contributions to the cultural formation of the Basque American society.

After beginning the research with the interviews in Idaho, the quest for information subsequently took me to the old country. I received a grant from the Ansotegui-Fereday Memorial Scholarship in Boise, Idaho, to study in the Basque Country with scholars Teresa del Valle and Gorka Aulestia. In addition to formal classes in Basque anthropology, language, and history, I was introduced to everyday life in San Sebastian, a Basque town very close to the French border, by an informative Basque woman who had lived in Pocatello, Idaho. While in Idaho, her Basque husband was employed by the Union Pacific Railroad. They retired in the old country to be near extended family. After returning to America, I conducted further interviews with over a hundred Basque American women in Idaho, Nevada, California, and Oregon. Though some of the women I interviewed were professionals, most of the individuals were homemakers whose names had not appeared in books or newspapers, and who had not demonstrated an active interest in public affairs. Among my subjects were sheepherders' and ranchers' wives, who performed traditional supporting roles in those operations, and many who had worked in or even owned boarding houses. These were quiet tradition-bearers. However, not all of their husbands or fathers were sheepherders; among the spouses and fathers of the women interviewed were business men, professors, lawyers, pharmacists, engineers, and construction contractors.

Beginning with the early interviews, I quickly discovered that the women were powerful preservers of their cultural heritage and had no intention of being "just Americans." The women have been instrumental in shaping, transmitting, and maintaining contemporary Basque American culture. They have stories to tell and strong voices with which to tell them. The women have conceptualized their ethnicity, with its inherited folkloric culture and behavior, and have established it in this country with syncretized folkways, mores, and even newly invented traditions. Cherished stories are often transmitted at kitchen and dining room tables where, following sacred blessings sometimes spoken in the language of their homeland, the shaping narratives of past generations are passed to the next one. The ancient Basque language is a key to the maintenance of the Basque culture in the old country, but in the United States elements in addition to the language bind the ongoing Basque American community together. Those elements are what the women want to share. These are Americans with strong Basque roots who are eager to have a spotlight on their contributions to North America.

When news of the study I had undertaken spread among some networks of women in Idaho, Montana, Nevada, and California, I began receiving short personal histories in the mail, phone calls, and occasional newspaper clippings about various women who had contributed to the Basque American culture in positive ways. I have taken those stories and sometimes combined them with published and unpublished sources of information to strengthen and expand the record and its presentation. I have tried not to distort their voices with my own.

I am a folklorist, but I have learned to identify myself as a cultural historian or ethnographer to the individuals I interview because of the confusion about what folklorists do. I learned quickly, through experience, that when I identified myself as a folklorist, there was an automatic assumption that I was collecting only traditional stories, myths, legends, and folktales. Perhaps there is a necessity of reconfiguring the name of our field (Kirshenblatt-Gimblett 1995, 134). The women were often relieved to learn that I was interested in their personal narratives because many of them knew no folktales from their homeland.

The text is divided into three chapters and an afterword. Chapter one establishes historical background and context for the old world Basques. Language and folkloric elements are discussed and traditional female occupations in the old country considered. The chapter concludes with narratives of women's immigration experiences. Chapter two describes women's life in the boarding houses and Basque hotels of the

American West. It includes narratives from sheepmen's wives and daughters and from Basque American women in modern occupations. Chapter three discusses the traditions and folklore of the Basque American women and men, who are determined to keep alive the soul of their inherited cultural mores while participating fully in American society. Inventions, oral traditions, customs, rites of passage, Basque American festivals, and other examples of cultural maintenance will illustrate how many of the cultural and folkloric elements discussed in chapter one have taken on a Basque American character, revealing Basque American identity.

The afterword presents an overview of the Basque American culture in the United States, postulates projections toward the future, and considers broader meanings and influences that the study of this group and their cultural adaptations may have. We know that societies and cultures do not stand alone but are composed of many voices and influences. Critically examining how cultural inventions, folkloric traditions, and social adaptations of the Basque American people led them to become "quintessential Americans," as they have been called in the Western states, may point a way for other cultural groups to follow.

Virginia Argoitia, Sparks, Nevada.

1

Grandfather's Chair

Virginia Argoitia, of Sparks, Nevada, was born in Wyoming to parents from Marquina in the province of Vizcaya, in the Basque Country. Like many Basque Americans, she has made several trips to the old country to visit relatives and to simply enjoy the unique beauty of the small country at the inner elbow of Spain and France. On one of her trips, Virginia was taken to the ancient sanctuary of Arretxinaga near her natal village. There, her relatives lifted a chair from a rail on the wall and set it before her. The family name had been carved in the back of the chair, and Virginia was told that it had been made by one of her grandfathers. In one position the chair served as a kneeling rail; in the other, it was a well-worn seat. Virginia knelt on the rail of this cherished family relic and told me that she felt a comfortable familiarity. She said: "You don't feel like you are in a foreign country. You feel like you belong there." (8 June 1993). The reality of her inherited identity as a Basque came to her and she knew, in a flood of emotion, that she was a part of her homeland.

Historical Background and Context

Basque history has taken place within a country so beautiful that to some it has seemed almost like a fairyland. There are ancient mountain forests, hidden caves and icy mountain streams, Christian grottos, and ruins of ancient Roman roads. The foamy, blue Sea of Biscay, abundant with sea life, roils ceaselessly onto craggy rocks and clean sand beaches. Picturesque white stucco farmsteads, with their required-by-ordinance red tile roofs, nestle on tiny well-tended plots of land and literally dot the hills and the valleys. Cosmopolitan cities, with the exquisite and varied architectural styles of nineteenth and twentieth century Europe, enhanced by contemporary sculpture and architecture, flourish along the northern coast. These cities are centers of both Basque and Spanish economy. Industry and commerce there have drawn workers from all over Spain. The Basque Country is rich with tradition and folklife reflective of the three topographical regions of the land: coastal, mountain, and plains. The primary occupations of the people are related to coastal fishing, industry, and small-scale farming.

The country is divided between northern Spain and southern France, with three provinces on the French side of the border and four provinces on the Spanish side. The Basque people who live there prefer not to think of that division as a border. The Pyrenees Mountains form a natural partition between Spain and France, and the Basques would rather conceptualize the rugged, natural disruption between the two nations as a frontier. Their traditional view of their country is as one whole nation that encompasses seven provinces. This concept is referred to as *Zazpiak Bat* (seven in one), a slogan I observed often on fine ceramic plates, artfully decorated mugs, and enameled wall plaques in many of the Basque American homes I visited. Those artifacts are abundantly available both at shops in the old country and at fairs and festivals held in the western American states.

"White stucco farmsteads dot the hills and valleys."

The *Zazpiak Bat* coat-of-arms of the Basque Country represents seven provinces in one.

To display them in one's American home denotes the pride of heritage that many Basque Americans share. There are ancient traditions that wind back into the late medieval period suggesting that many Basques considered themselves a notch above people in neighboring countries. The origin of these traditions, *fueros*, will be explained in the following history.

Much of the material in this discussion was taken from readings, lectures, notes and discussions of Basque and Spanish history which I studied in San Sebastian in 1990, under the direction of Gorka Aulestia, a lexicographer, literary historian, and an internationally known and respected Basque scholar.

Aulestia gave me several of his unpublished essays and permission to use them. Citations are entered when the sources are identifiable. This material is important in order to enable the reader to comprehend the source of ethnic pride and cultural uniqueness that many of the Basques, both in the old country and the United States, find so natural to maintain.

Basque Americans have been accused by some non-Basques as being clannish and aloof. They themselves have reminded me that for many of them, one personal offense is usually all they allow. The Basques have an ancient culture with mysterious origins, and they continue to practice and keep alive one of the most obscure languages on earth. It has no real affinity with any other known language, though speculation about the root source is rampant. Through would-be conquerors, wars, famines, political instability, and blatant persecutions, these people and their language have survived intact. The cultural tenacity demonstrated in saving their language from outside corruption, and their determined pride of origin, are elements of the legacy that many Basques in the United States, even to the third and fourth generation, try to preserve.

The prehistoric cave at Santimamiñe, in the Basque Country, is perhaps the earliest evidence of Basque energy. Though the purpose of the cave and its paintings remains a mystery, it demonstrates the presence of an intelligent, creative people in the Middle Paleolithic age. Cro-Magnon man, discovered in the same general area of this and other caves, is perhaps also linked to this early people. Some Basques claim to be direct descendants of these early hunters and gatherers.

According to most scholars, the oldest or first known invaders of Spain were the Indo-Europeans. These were a people the Romans called Iberians—hence the Iberian Peninsula, which extends to the north of Spain beyond the Pyrenees and into what is now France. Historians think that the Celts were among the next to come to the area, followed by the Phoenicians, and then the Greeks, the Romans, and the Goths. Each attempted but none really succeeded in conquering the Vascones, or Basques. Though the Romans left behind some Latin suffixes and prefixes which were grafted into the Basque language, no invader could penetrate their country, their culture, or their language unless invited. Their natural protection was the rugged, mountainous region and their Basques' intrepid ability to out-maneuver any potential invader. The country eventually evolved into the seven provinces of today: Alava, Vizcaya, Guipúzcoa, and Navarra in Spain, and Labourd, Basse Navarre, and Soule in France. In A.D. 711, Arabs arrived and overwhelmed the Goths, but they too were unable to entirely conquer the Basques.

In the year A.D. 778, Charlemagne, king of the Franks, raised a large army and crossed the Pyrenees hoping to undermine Arab unity. He led his troops to Arab-held Zaragoza, found the city gates closed, and decided not to attack. Instead he leveled Pamplona, another Arab-held city, and then crossed the Pyrenees at Roncevilles. During that crossing, an army attacked Charlemagne's rear guard and a number of noblemen were lost including Roland, the subject of the famous ballad, *Chanson de Roland* (Douglass and Bilbao 1975, 41). According to the Arab historian S. M. Imamuddin, the attacking army was made up of Basques (Garatea 1990, 14).

Historically called "Vascones" or "Gascones," the Basques established a reputation for pagan brutality, violence, and ferocity remarkable even in the Dark Ages. The Basque war cry, the *irrintzi*, now the subject of competitions at festivals both in the old country and in America, struck terror in the hearts of many would-be invaders. It sounds like a derisive laugh which then changes to a horse's shrill neigh and then to a wolf's howl; it ends like the expiring notes of a jackass's bray. The Basque's physical strength, stamina, and guerrilla tactics, coupled with the rugged terrain of their homeland, presented impossible odds for their enemies. Rodney Gallop, anthropologist, quotes seventh century Saint Amand, who fled to the Basques after a court scandal, as saying that he had escaped to "these tribes among whom he hoped to win the palms of martyrdom on account of their ferocity" (1970, 12). Gallop states that several centuries later Saint Eusiba, a native of the Basque Country trying to practice his religion there, "was said to have been devoted to God among people given over to diabolical practices" (1970, 11).

Sancho Garces III, called Sancho El Mayor, king of the province of Navarra from about A.D. 1004 to 1035, entered into alliances with the French and with the Banu Qus, a powerful family of Hispano-Roman stock who had become Islamic. He built a great empire to the north, east, and west. He avoided defeat by not challenging the south, which was still occupied and defended by powerful Moors. During his reign, the basic area of the current Basque Country was defined. During his reign also, the doors of culture, travel, and literacy were opened; the religion and culture of France and Italy were observed and emulated (Bard 1982, 40).

More importantly, the *foral* base, or *fueros* as mentioned above, laws to protect consistently the rights of male Basque citizens according to the sensibilities of the times, began to be established during Sancho's reign. These unique laws are a part of what some contemporary Basques in France and Spain still live and fight for. Protective, fair, expedient, and sometimes peculiarly quaint, the *fueros*, combined with traditions of collective nobility such as exemption from military conscription for all citizens, are the very heart of symbolic Basque nationalism.

Quoting Julien Vinson, who was the doyen of Basque studies until his death in the mid-twentieth century, Gallop writes: "The *fueros*, provincial and local, grew into a legislative code consisting of 'the sum total of laws and regulation dealing with all subjects from the political constitution and principal legislative measures to the smallest details of everyday life.'"

The *fueros* of Vizcaya, for instance, included prescriptions concerning the manner of mourning the dead:

> "No person ... may make moan, tearing his hair, or scratching his head (*sic*) nor lament in song ... under penalty of 1000 maravedia ... ." Some of the *fueros* were pure folklore and consecrated pagan customs. There is a series of prescriptions in which animals are treated as reasoning beings; others defining the obligation of a citizen to furnish his neighbor with fire; and others providing for judicial ordeals by duel, by candle (the party whose candle first burnt out lost his case), by fire and by water. (14).

The rudiments of the laws were in place at the time of Sancho El Mayor's death. The Basque self-perception of nobility as part of their cultural heritage arises directly out of the *fueros*. According to Roger Collins, probable patterns for "the earliest Spanish *fueros* or charters of immunity were granted by lords, such as its count, to settlers in Castile" as early as the 950s (1990, 169). In Guipúzcoa and Vizcaya, provinces never conquered by the Moors, nobility was granted to all inhabitants by law. In Vizcaya, the only requirement for a grant of nobility was that of birth to parents who resided in that province. In Navarra and the French provinces, inhabitants of villages and even whole regions were sometimes ennobled at once. One of the most important and cherished privileges granted to the Basques by the *fueros* was their exemption from military duty outside the boundaries of their own provinces. In other words, no neighboring country (specifically Spain or France) could conscript their services; consequently, they felt protected and somewhat ennobled by their exemption from common soldier duties. Also, under the *fueros*, Spanish troops were forbidden access to the Basque provinces.

Though not provable by written records, it is possible that democratic features of the laws emerged from very early Castillian traditions. Historian Roger Collins wrote that "as early as 956 A.D. there was evidence of democratic institutions in Castille" not unlike "self-governing institutions found in Guipúzcoa and Vizcaya in later centuries" (169). By A.D. 1212, northern Spain was finally rid of the Moorish occupation after a great Crusader victory at Las Navas de Tolosa. Because of Basque assistance in this victory, the consolidation and organization of the Basque Country began, and the *fueros* began to be exercised almost as a pure form of democracy (Clark 1979). By the end of the 17th century, each of the seven Basque provinces had forms of *fueros* which limited the interference of both Spain and France in Basque financial, political and legal affairs (Collins 1990, 267). Every member of the Basque society in Guipúzcoa, Vizcaya, part of Navarra, and the French provinces was protected by the *fueros*, and the representative courts in Guernica guaranteed legislated and protected civil rights to every citizen. Wealth or family heritage made no difference. The *fueros* provided full local autonomy to the Basque people and, "The king was not, as elsewhere, the owner of the land ..." (Gallop 1987, 15). The Basque people paid a fixed annual tribute to their monarch, but they were able to structure the payment of the tribute as they wished (Gallop 1987, 15). Each of the seven provinces administered the *fueros* independently, and assemblies elected in the provinces had varied types of representatives. In the Spanish provinces, the representatives were usually elected citizens; in Basse Navarre, they were representatives of the church; in Labourd, the representatives were mayors of Labourd's different communes (Gallop 1987, 16).

The concept of nobility guaranteed by the *fueros* was perceived as a moral goodness rather than a position of power. It was a sense of pride, of independence founded, in part, on the fact that the Basques protected themselves and were never forced to bow to the Moors. They considered themselves independent of the surrounding world (Spain and France), and for many Basques that concept continues to be a source of contemporary pride.

By A.D. 1512, the Catholic monarchs Ferdinand and Isabella set out to subjugate Navarra. Pushing the French aside, Ferdinand strengthened the area from his seat in Pamplona. "The establishment of a Spanish-French border in 1512 created divisiveness in the Basque area that lasted from the sixteenth century to the present" (Douglass and Bilbao 1975, 13). The Basque Country on the northern side of the Pyrenees, Basse Navarre and Soule, was formally organized as a part of France in 1620 by the Edict of Union issued at Pau by Louis XIII (Collins 1986, 263).

In the late 1700s, the French Revolution caused the *fors* or *fueros* to be abolished in France. The hated French Bourbon rule in Spain was overthrown in November of 1813, and the Navarran kingdom's autonomy and ancient *fueros* were reestablished by Ferdinand VII of Spain in August of 1814 (Hilton 1987, 27). Disillusionment with Ferdinand eventually caused Spain's first civil war from 1820 to 1823 (the Guerra Realista). Later, absolutists, royalists, constitutionalists, and liberals engaged in the First Carlist War. The Basques were primarily Carlists.

The Carlists supported Don Carlos, pretender to the Spanish throne, on the death of his brother Ferdinand VII in 1833. They supported the causes associated with his name: absolute monarchy, traditional Catholicism, and regional autonomy. Ancestors of women I interviewed fought in the Carlist civil wars, which were fought from 1834 to 1840 for the purpose of placing Don Carlos on the throne, and again from 1872 to 1876 to establish a monarchy. In addition to being traditionalist and devoutly Catholic, the Carlists believed that if they could gain power, they could maintain the rights and privileges of the ancient laws. However, the wars and the *fueros* were lost. The two Carlist wars resulted in the entire loss of the protection and rights of the ancient *fueros*. After 1876, the Basque culture underwent vast changes. Power over the Basques was taken by the central government in Madrid. Because they had lost their protections, privileges, and rights in the homeland, many young Basques began large migrations to North and South America. The loss of the Basques' traditional liberties and the forced introduction of the Spanish and French language and customs threatened the existence of a separate Basque culture.

In 1890, a political idealist named Sabino de Arana y Goiri, the son of an exiled Carlist, published a pamphlet called *Bizkaya por su Independencia*, which aroused the interest and nationalistic passion of the Basque people. Arana was the founder of the PNV, the *Partido Nacionalista Vasco*, or the Basque Nationalist Party. Arana was deeply disturbed by the influx of Spanish industrial workers into the Basque region. He realized that without resistance, the cherished language and customs of the Basques, preserved and practiced since antiquity, would be lost in the culture and language of the Spanish. With fervent hopes of saving the Basque culture and language from corruption and eventual loss, Arana was determined to protect, teach, and preserve it (Aulestia n.d.).

Sabino Arana's efforts reawakened a great desire among many Basques to preserve and retain their language, their cultural traditions, and what they perceived to be their lawful rights. The result of this nationalism, stirred up by Arana's idealistic political and religious views, was a climate of Spanish political oppression which resulted in forced migration for many of the Basque people (Aulestia n.d.). Basques continued to leave the country to join Basque friends and family members who had migrated earlier and who had already established themselves in communities, businesses, and homes in North, Central, and South America.

The years between 1890 and the beginning of the Spanish Civil War in 1936 were politically tumultuous. Anarchist terrorism rose throughout Spain, the interests of business and labor seemed irreconcilable, and there were political and economic problems in Spanish-occupied Morocco. In 1931, left and liberal groups took over the central government in Spain. The new defense minister, Manuel Asaña, became leader of the Republican left.

The Basques bid for home rule by supporting the Republican government. Their characteristic religious devotion, political isolation, and agricultural self-sufficiency allowed them to be independent, at least for a while. Navarra was part Basque and traditionally Roman Catholic and was still the homeland of many Carlists. In the divisive election of 1936, a struggle between the right, center, and left, the Basques had nine seats in the Congress of Deputies, the representative assembly in Madrid. General Emilio Mola, a Spanish nationalist and army commander in Pamplona, Navarra, arranged a military coup d'etat, ill-coordinated but with a goal of stopping leftist power, economic disaster, and social disorder. Navarra was a divided province, and he chose it as his base (Clark 1979).

General Mola and General Francisco Franco, who was soon named head of the nationalist government and generalissimo of the armed forces, began the overthrow of the Spanish government that led to the Spanish Civil War. The war raged throughout Spain from 1936 until 1939. Hugh Thomas states that, "In the spring of 1936, Mola and others sought to draw the Basque Nationalists away from their alliance with the left. Some arms were even made available to them" (Thomas 1986, 175). Though the Basques were more centrist than leftist and were distant from the quarrels of the south, their president and leader, José Antonio Aguirre, said they would "stand by the government of Madrid until the defeat of fascism" (Thomas 1986, 430). The Basques were defeated in 1937. By siding with the Republican forces in the war, the Basques were antagonists of the Franco regime. Franco established a specific reign of terror and suppression against Basque nationals which lasted from

1935 until his death in 1975 (Eiguren 1972, 70–111). Thus, unleashed upon them was first the fury and terror of Mola's power and then Franco's persecution. The stories of the Basque resistance are legion.

Some of my informants described the horror of living in the Basque Country during the Civil War. The war remains in the collective memory of many Basque American men and women, whether they experienced it first-hand or vicariously through relatives or friends. The aerial bombing of Guernica on a Monday afternoon market day (known to have been performed by German Nazi fighter planes as practice for later aerial raids in Europe), the heroic but tragic battle in the Bay of Biscay harbor between three trawlers and the Spanish ship *Canarias*, and the refusal of the people in Bilbao to succumb to starvation tactics levied upon them by Mola and Franco are incidents that have inspired artists, poets, and the *bertsolariak* (or Basque troubadours) to extol the bravery and fortitude of their people.

Franco died in 1975; however, violence and persecution were not to come to an abrupt end at the close of his dictatorship. Resistance to the central government of Spain is still high among a few nationalists in the Basque Country as evidenced by the plethora of hostile graffiti on many large public buildings, bridges, and walls. Some Spanish-worded street signs and markers throughout the Basque nation have been marred with a coil spray of black paint; frequently lettered in below the coil, in amateur script, will be the same information written in the Basque language.

While I was in San Sebastian in the summer of 1990, the Bank of Spain was bombed and its first floor largely destroyed shortly before dawn. The public assumed that the incident, rather than an attempt to injure or kill anyone, was a show of presence, strength, and terror by some violent pro-nationalist group. I observed armed Spanish *Guardia Civils* (Civil Guards) stationed throughout San Sebastian; they appeared to be intense and watchful.

One Nevada Basque American woman stated (anony-
mous, interview, 11 June 1993) that the homes of her father and
father-in-law, in Vizcaya, were still searched now and then
because both men had been incarcerated in the past for political
resistance. In the middle 1980s, the last time she, her husband,
and her children spent a few weeks on her father's *baserri* (homestead), one of her boys left a toy gun, a pistol, behind by accident. It was on a table beside the bed he used. After the family
left to return to the United States, the Spanish police arrived at
the door and demanded to search the house. When they found
the toy gun in the drawer of the nightstand, they confiscated it
and reprimanded the old man for having such a thing in his
house. The woman conjectured that a neighbor had seen the
gun, mistaken it for a real one, and reported it to the Spanish
authorities.

The central government in Spain has successfully established a constitutional monarchy based on democracy, a respect
for law, and a capitalist economy. The Basques have been granted
representation in the *Cortes*, or Spanish government, and a measured autonomy; however, the threat of Basque insurgency is not
one that the leaders in Madrid will ever take lightly. Many
Basques continue to oppose the Spanish presence in their
provinces not only because of Spanish influence on their ancient
language, but also because the Basque people seem to differ from
surrounding European populations in the frequency of certain
blood types.

There is extensive literature supporting the unique blood
hypothesis, and in 1969, William C. Boyd hypothesized that a
high incidence of the RH negative RH factor and an unusually
low incidence of blood type B characterized clear descent of contemporary Basques from a lost race of Iberians (1057–64).
Admitting a wide range of speculation on this issue, the classic
text representing Basques in America, *Amerikanuak: Basques in
the New World*, by anthropologist William A. Douglass and historian Jon Bilbao, states that the Basques in northern Spain

remained, "over a relatively long period of time, a small and somewhat isolated breeding population" (1975, 10). In that Old World region, according to Douglass and Bilbao, there is a high rate of occurrence of the Rh negative factor, and a low occurrence of blood type B; both occur more frequently there than in the rest of the world.

In 1992, M. I. Arrieta and others reported additional evidence of differences between the Basque population and other European populations. This team of biologists examined the skin on the fingertips and palms of unrelated normal individuals from eight Basque valleys (Uribe, Guernica, Marquina, Arratia, Durango, Deba, Urola, and Salazar). These individuals each had eight great-grandparents born in the same valley. Diverse dermatoglyphic differentiation demonstrated that the Basques examined differed from other Europeans examined and from each other, valley to valley. These studies reflect the ongoing efforts to trace the movements of people by examining genetic characteristics. "Drift [or movement] could have been the evolutionary force most important in promoting diversity among the Basque valley populations because the populations are small and isolated by mountains" (Arrieta et. al. 1992, 714).

Individual efforts continue to challenge the hypothesis of Basque genetic uniqueness. In an article entitled "Basque Culture is Unique," published in the *Times-News*, Twin Falls, Idaho, 1 June 1991, it was reported that Hohn B. Graham, a North Carolinae genetic researcher, tested individuals whose four grandparents were of Basque origin. He concluded that Basques are "run-of-the-mill Europeans, genetically speaking." Gloria Lejardi, a Basque American woman residing in Homedale, Idaho, responded to Graham's findings and was quoted as follows, "Culturally, I know that I'm unique. I think that's what matters most to any of the European cultures." It is the Basque women's unwavering perception of uniqueness, for whatever reasons, and cultural members' efforts to reify that perception that are important in this story. The findings of science were inconclusive, but the uncontrovertible "lore" of uniqueness remains and continues to shape Basque identity.

In addition to the unique and untraceable Basque language and speculated blood anomalies, scholars have investigated what some have felt to be visible physical characteristics unique to the Basque population. Several individuals I interviewed, not genetic scholars, stated firmly that they believed the Basque skeletal structure to be evidence that the Basques directly descended from the Cro-Magnon people. The cultural folklore claims that Basque skulls have markedly long jaw bones. They have also mentioned what they observe to be particularly thick musculature in the necks of men and elongated torsos, long arms, and generally, short legs.

Studies popular at the turn of the nineteenth century speculated about specific bone structures and their connections to race, but they fell out of fashion because of more sophisticated, and accurate, studies in genetics. As late as 1939, Carlton Coon of Harvard University quoted an earlier study that suggested that Basque skeletons from the Bronze Age found in the ancient dolmens of Guipúzcoa represented skull and bone types similar to those of contemporary Basques. Coon states: "The Basques, through inbreeding, ethnic solidarity, and the possession of a recognized national ideal type, have developed a characteristic physiognomy, the essential features of which are nasal prominence and a prominence and a narrowness of the median sagittal facial segment, and of the mandible" (1939, 503).

A more recent text, in considering the genetic composition of European populations, discusses the effect of neolithic bands in the Basque regions on genetic composition. (Cavalli-Sforza, Piazza, and Menozzi 1993). Irrespective of the amount of empirical evidence, many Basques believe that they are genetically unique. The essential point is not that there is a *truth* concerning these issues, but rather that the *belief* that there are unique physical markers reifies and legitimizes that concept. The belief, an invented and shaped narrative, has been repeated and passed on and thereby has become a part of the collective Basque lore.

Before closing this section on historical background and context, it is important to consider discussion of the Basque language. In 1918 at the close of World War I, Euskaltzaindia, or the Academy of the Basque Language was founded. The hardest problem the academy had to resolve was the profusion of dialects. For instance, according to lexicographer Gorka Aulestia, there are at least 47 correct ways to say "butterfly" (Aulestia 1978, 4). Mikel Zarete (1933–1979), a Vizcayan writer, wrote a poem which metaphorically expressed his feelings and frustrations about the profusion of Basque dialects. Aulestia included the poem in his essay about Zarete, and it is included here in both Basque and in Aulestia's English translation:

Piny gegueguz	Pine Forest
pinuturiko	planted
pinudi ...	with too many pines.
Bageniezazu ...	———
lekizkizueke ...	———
Hau larria!	What a mess!
Gaizki dut eztarria	My throat hurts.
Zinatekete	———
likizkizueke ...	———
Aditz	Damned
bortitz	synthetic
madarikatua! ...	Verb!
Arnurna Sare	Stupid
alua!	Spider's web!
Ez irten ez sartu,	One cannot leave,
	Nor can one enter
Ezin irten ez sartu,	One cannot breathe.
Gintzaiskizuekeen	———
geniezazkizxuekeen	———
Hainbeste era ... ,	Why

zertarako?	So many verb forms?
Zuka, hika	Formal speech,
	familiar speech
(To ta no)	differing when dealing with
	a man or a woman
Hau amets iguingarri!	What a repulsive dream!
Zer da hori?	What is this?
Traste zagarren museo	A museum of antiquities,
aitonen mausoleo	A mausoleum of ancestors ...
Kanposantua?	A cemetery?
Muturaren Kantua? ...	The song of mutes?
Egin	Carry out
nirekin	with me
presaka	as soon as possible
entresaka	the thinning of the Forest. (29–31)

As with the fierce independent attitude of the small mil-itant nationalistic faction that is active in the Basque Country, strong feelings still exist concerning the way the Basque language can best be preserved. Conflict and sometimes violence in the Basque Country continues, in part, about language. Spanish has infiltrated all of the Spanish Basque provinces. Spanish is spoken on the street, and the Catholic mass is commonly conducted in Spanish. It is a little difficult, at least in San Sebastian, to find the mass being said in Basque. Linda White, a professor of Basque studies at the University of Nevada, Reno, has noted: "The Basque people are putting forth a phenomenal effort to save their minority language in the face of overwhelming cultural saturation in the Spanish tongue ... the *ikastolak*, or schools where all the subjects are taught in the Basque language, are a tribute to the Basque people and their love for their language" (Lecture, 14 June 1990).

In the contemporary Basque Country, a child's training and education from the nursery through the university can now be conducted entirely in Basque. Organizations formed to establish various types of Basque language schools (*ikastolak*) have become numerous in the last twenty years. Strong feeling surrounding the combined or unified dialect called *Batua* still exist because some Basques resent the potential loss of their distinctive dialects. In order to preserve the language though, linguists realized that a consensus had to be defined. Basque could not be taught unless it was unified. *Batua* is the primary form of Basque language currently taught in the old country and the United States.

Myths and Folkloric Elements of the Old Culture

The Abbé Diharce de Bidassouet wrote in his *Histoire des Cantabres* that Basque was "the original language spoken by the Creator" (Gallop 1970, 2). There were others, Gallop says, that held a "widespread conviction that Basque, if not divine, was at least the first human tongue" (2). Still others posit that surely Basque was the original language before the scattering of people at the Tower of Babel. Another Abbé, Dominique Lahetjuzan (1766–1818), wrote prolifically about the divinity of the Basque language, and even suggested that "the Basque word *laranja:* orange (which happens to be only a mispronunciation of the Spanish *naranja)* is derived from Basque roots meaning 'the fruit which was first eaten.' Hence the orange and not the apple was the cause of Adam's downfall" (Gallop 1970, 4). Theories and humorous anecdotes about Basque origins and the cherished language abound in the Basque culture both in the old country and in the United States. The one I heard most frequently was about the Devil. Because the language was so difficult, several informants told me, Satan was not able to learn it. That, therefore, is the reason the Basques are so good. Satan did not know their language and therefore could not tempt them.

"According to Father Barandiarán, one of the great experts on Basque matters, this is a culture which goes back 50,000 years" (Sevilla 1990, xii). When Christianity was introduced,

around A.D. 900, there is little doubt that some of the pagan practices were kept. One tradition that threads its way through many
Basque myths and folktales is that of the mountain figure Mari.
This female cultural force represents ancient beliefs and though
everyone who seems to know about her agrees that she is a woman,
her descriptions and activities vary widely. Some individuals who
claim sightings say that she appears as an elegant lady who holds a
palace in her hands; others say she wears a long red tunic; some say
that they have seen her crossing the sky at a high speed; sometimes
she appears in fire, and many believe that she lives in a cave.
Others believe that she is surrounded by animals; sometimes she
appears as a tree and has a halo around her head like a full moon,
and some say she is surrounded by a rainbow. If one encounters
Mari in the woods or near her cave, and if that one touches or is
touched by her, it is said that the victim will be transposed into
Mari. It is said that she has many names and shapes and extraordinary powers.

Teresa del Valle lectured on Mari and her meanings in
San Sebastian 1 August 1990. In that lecture she stated that the
tales and traditions about Mari belong to both the realm of myth
and the community of humans. Mari constantly presents oppo-
sites. In the Basque culture and others, del Valle suggested, individuals are confronted with "frequent examples of contradictions."
Reflecting the culture, Mari moves between black and white
forces, and a person might consult Mari about a problem because
she sees both sides objectively. She can enter dreams and sometimes help resolve problems in the dreamer's subconscious. The
lore about visiting her is precise. If you enter a cave to consult
her, you must enter with your face forward. As you leave the
cave, you must continue to face her. It is said that she not only
has the knowledge of the "yes" and the "no," but she can feed
herself on the "yes" and "no." In Mari's cave are golden objects,
but if they are removed it is said that they turn into garbage. The
moral of that story, del Valle said, was that "Mari's wealth can
only be converted to nothing." One of the students asked if Mari

was a persona of the Virgin Mary. In response, del Valle suggested that there are similar traditions in other cultures, but that unlike the Virgin Mary, Mari is not a character you would want to be very close to.

Joe V. Eiguren, in his text *The Basque History: Past and Present*, wrote that the earliest information about the Basques came from Strabo, a writer born in Rome in 57 B.C. Strabo, a keen descriptive ethnographer, recorded some revealing characteristics and practices of these ancient people:

> From the writings of Strabo we have learned that the Basques did not have much to do with other people of the peninsula. Their life was austere; they ate dried acorns, cow and goat meat, cow fat, fish and legumes. They drank water only one-third of the year and a sour wine, called "txakoli," the rest of the year. For festive meals they sat around a large circular table and the places of honor were occupied by the elders. Entertainment was usually furnished by the young dancers of the group, who danced separately from one another to the lively tune of a vertical flute and a drum.
>
> The men were usually attired in trousers and a black, smock-like loose coat. They were always bareheaded, even in combat. The women wore bright colored clothing. They did not have a national currency and they exchanged goods, food, or labor in their business transactions. Criminals or murderers were punished by death, usually being thrown from a precipice or cliff. (Eiguren 1972, 23–24)

Eiguren explained further that killing family members to prevent their falling into the hands of enemies was common, and further, if captured and hung on a cross for execution, the Basques "died singing contemptuously" (Eiguren 1972, 24).

The Basque people traditionally perceive themselves as strong morally, mentally, and physically. Three words that I heard mentioned frequently while I was studying with the Basques in Spain were: *adur, indarra, sendotasuna.* Transmitted through vernacular exchange between teachers and students, parents and children, and friend to friend, these concepts seem to define a sense of strength and competence. *Adur* is a positive or negative force which can be projected on a person or object. It seems to imply an outside power, sometimes malignant, and it is primarily associated with some sort of a negative feminine capacity. What might be referred to in the United States as feminine wiles or feminine mystique could be called *adur* in the Basque Country. *Indarra* and *sendotasuna* identify differing types of inner strengths. *Indarra* is biological; *sendotasuna* is a kind of strength that seems to convey confidence to people outside of one's self. The transmission and repetition of these concepts in everyday conversation furthers the sense of pride and confidence that the Basques try to maintain.

Both in the United States and in the Basque Country, I have often heard both women and men refer to an ancient Basque matriarchy and its legacy of strength and power to the Basque women. Many Basque women are powerful in their domestic spheres, guiding the family in religion, deciding in which house or apartment the family will live, which schools the children will attend, and how the family income will be used. Most of the women I interviewed believed in a legacy of inner strength which they most often credited to faith and prayer. Teresa del Valle debunks the ideology of an ancient matriarchy among the Basques almost entirely and suggests that it is, perhaps, a contemporary male-constructed myth. Noting that the matriarchal myth *has* been widely accepted among the Basques, both male and female, she suggests that A. Ortiz Oses, the philosopher and anthropologist who has published much on the subject, has used an argument "based on tenuous anthropological data and extensive interpretation" (1990, 28).[3] Further,

A stained glass window at the government center in Guernica. Photograph by
Gloria Tortoricaguena, from the 1997 North American Basque Organization
calendar.

"The myth serves to justify at an ideal level the traditional role
of women which encloses her in a narrow and restricted world
with limited rewards" (1990, 31). Though perhaps only in
meaningful jesting, the folkloric concept of the power of the
Basque women persists.

The center of Basque Old World democracy was
Guernica, now the seat of the Basque autonomous government.
There are stories and traditions attached to this beloved city of
the Basques. Because visiting and even retiring there is not
uncommon among Basque Americans, I was told that Basque
American tourists often have chance encounters with old friends
on the streets and in the restaurants of Guernica. When I toured
Guernica, I went to the central government building and viewed
the magnificent stained glass windows that enclose the ceiling.

There, in jewel-like color, is a brilliant panorama of highlights of the history of the Basque Country. Not unlike the great cathedrals of the world, one can read significant events and legends in the glass. The *junta*, or government of the province of Vizcaya, used to meet in Guernica under an oak tree near a pseudo-Greek temple which still stands. The famous oak in the courtyard, one of the seven symbols of the Basque provinces, has been replaced by young saplings over time. I was told there that one of the saplings had been planted in Boise, Idaho, a town considered a sister city to Guernica. "Guernica'ko Arbola," unofficially the national anthem of the Basque Country, is sung at many Basque functions in the old country.

Customary celebrations in the Basque Country originate in Catholic beliefs. It is difficult to understand the beginning and end of the people's emotions, but the feelings at festival and celebrations run deep. Most *fiestas* and celebrations are repeated each year in an annual cycle. At Christmas time, gifts are exchanged on January 6. There is also a celebration at that time called the *Olantero*, which features a figure representing the rural area dressed in a blue shirt and trousers. His figure is lifted in a chair and carried. The *Olantero* celebrates the coming of the Christians to the Basque Country, but the figure also symbolically represents fighting for the culture's old ways. It is interesting that this figure can be used in different ways and be interpreted to have various messages. Easter is another important celebration, but most important is the week before Easter. Known as Holy Week, it is one of masses and fasting during which devout Catholics spend extra hours in prayer. There are many winter carnivals with rich displays of color and music. As in countries around the world, family relationships are renewed at holidays and celebrations.

In San Sebastian, Spain, I observed and participated in a week-long festival held in honor of Saint Ignatius Loyola, the patron saint of the Basques. Figures of giants (*gigantes*) and big-heads (*cabezudos*) appeared frequently on the streets and in the

Giants and bigheads on parade. Drawing by the author, based on a photograph by Maite Gorrindo, from the 1999 North American Basque Organization calendar.

parades. They were actually teenaged boys dressed up and performing as ludicrous clowns. The giants wore the garish clothing of a quasi king and queen; walking on stilts, they towered above everyone in the crowd. Their heads were formed of papier mâché, and they presented grotesque images of adult men and women. The bigheads were also dressed in colorful clothing that was baggy and casual. Their heads were enormous, with hideous smiling faces on them; they represented naughty children. Though the giants seemed benign and just wandered around dancing or marching in the frequent spontaneous parades, the bigheads carried padded white clubs (*porras*) or white balloons filled with water, and they chased girls and pretty women. When they caught up with one, they would hit her with the club or throw the balloon and then run away laughing and shouting insults.

These motifs are common at festivals around the Basque Country; the figures represent rebellion against authority. There are many levels of meaning to the figures, and the giant/bighead tradition is also common in Europe. According to S. Brandes, the padded clubs represent phalli, and the abuse of the females represents aggressive sex (Brandes 1990, 32). I was reminded of the strongly male-dominated traditions of the Basques in northern Spain, which are mediated by the great influence women have in the home and family sphere. An alternative though not conflicting hypothesis is that the giants represent the parental figures of Spanish authority, and the bigheads symbolically represent the resistance of the autonomous Basque Country.

During the St. Ignatius Loyola festival in San Sebastian, a mock bullfight was held, which was a travesty for both the participants and the bull. Scheduled to begin at six in the evening, it was nearly seven when it began. The bullfighters were young men whose ages ranged from twelve to eighteen or so, and they appeared to be quite drunk. A small bull was awkwardly released from the back of a pick-up truck, and then it was pushed into a ring of metal barriers. The boys, two at a time, poked at the bull with wooden sticks, shouted curses, and waved red and blue handkerchiefs. The helpless, confused animal was forced to run between cans and broken bottles of beer and to receive jabs from the foolish boys. The festival again seemed to be a forum for release of normally constrained aggression.

In spite of the rough play described above, the vast majority of Basques are a peace-loving people and many continue to faithfully practice the Roman Catholic religion. It has been noted that Basques, whether in America or in the old country, do not consider a meal complete without the presence of bread and wine. The combination of bread and wine may be rooted in largely forgotten rituals from early days. Sandra Ott, in her book about the French Basques of Sainte-Engrâce, discusses an ancient Basque custom of communal ritual responsibility for breads used at church or given to first of closest neighbors. To not take part in the custom was almost unthinkable. The *ogi benedi-datia* (blessed bread) custom meant that various households took turns baking and furnishing this homely food to neighbors and the church.[4]

Juan Garetea, a Basque priest whose parish is in Twin Falls, Idaho, shared (telephone interview, 15 November 1989) an old Spanish Basque custom that was practiced faithfully in his parents' home, Lekeito, Vizcaya, Spain. He feels the tradition might explain, at least in part, the significance of the required bread and wine at Basque meals. He first stated a prayer:

A Chea Den,
A Chiniu,
A Spiritu Santiun,
Amen.[5]

In the name of the Father,
And of the Son,
And of the Holy Spirit,
Amen.

And then he explained that with these ancient Christian words and the sign of the cross, the father of a religious family in the Basque Country of Spain blessed freshly baked bread on Christmas Eve. With the blessing completed, he broke the bread and gave a piece of it to each family member present. Then *etxekoandrea* (the mother of the house) wrapped the bread carefully and took it to the kitchen to be hidden away until the next Advent season. By practicing this family ritual, the family believed that they had guaranteed both spiritual and physical sustenance for the coming year. The following Advent season, the mother of the house prepared a soup or stew and used the bread from the previous year to thicken it. New bread was baked, and the ritual was again repeated. Father Garetea said that he has been in the United States for twenty-four years, but, he said sadly, this was only one of the many beautiful family rituals which were already being abandoned in Spain before he left.

When I observed them in 1990, Basque weddings in San Sebastian seemed to have the same characteristics as most American Catholic weddings. Robert Laxalt, well-known Basque American novelist, described Basque village weddings which followed old patterns and began with an afternoon wedding in the Catholic church. Then, "while their clans went on to the restaurant where the wedding supper was to be, the couple went alone to the cemetery." The couple looked "upon the cold grey place where one day they would lie together in death," and then they proceeded to the restaurant. With the bride attired in white and the groom and most of the guests dressed in black, the blending of the two families would take place amid cheerful toasts of wine and restrained partaking of foods. Some of the men would play cards and talk, and in time, the singing of the Basque songs began. It was not unusual for the men of the two families to sing verses back and forth, but, as Laxalt writes, "In this too, there was a measuring." The families took their time, and carefully measured their words and behavior before the uniting of the two clans really took place. Later in the evening, after the restraint of the two families was broken by wine and familiar conversation, the bride and groom led the entire wedding party and guests in a unified serpentine line that "swirled ... out into the darkness of the village street. There, with snapping fingers and flying feet and piercing yells, they formed a circle that dipped and rose"; and symbolically, the two families were united into one (1972, 88).

The folk dance is a common part of Basque culture. In the streets of Pamplona after the bullfights, spirited dancing of the *jota* takes place among friends and strangers. With one arm held in the air, and the other hooked to someone else, spontaneous dancing erupts in small groups as people leave the arena. The dance is ancient and most of the people take part at least for a little while. After a bullfight I attended there, I was drawn into street dancing by strangers and quickly learned that participant observation with the Basques, here or there, means to twirl as part of the joyful *jota*. One young Basque man who gently grabbed my arm in the Pamplona street asked if this were my first time at the festival of San Fermin. Our communication took a few minutes, but I finally conveyed that it was. With that, he took a wine soaked towel and generously sloshed my face on both sides. Laughingly he said, "Welcome to San Fermin!" And then chased off after his friends.

The bullfight itself is a folkloric event that has continued for centuries in the Basque Country, and in the *Fiesta del Toro*, the bull is the most important part. Ritualized activities involving man against beast, tradition, art, life and death, and even masculine (the bull) and feminine (the *matadore*) elements play themselves out season after season. The San Fermin festival in Pamplona begins with the *encierro*, or running of the bulls early in the morning. It is perceived as a rite of passage for young Basque males, though men of varied ages take part. It again denotes the strength or *indarra* of the Basque male.

Another tradition in the old country are the *bertsolaris* or versifiers. These singers can be male or female, and like the male singers Laxalt described at the wedding, the tradition is that they sing, improvising and creating rhymed verses as they sing back and forth between themselves. There are keen competitions among *bertsolaris*, and the art itself winds far back into time. Many of these talented and inventive artists are greatly loved and honored by the Basque people.

Besides lively celebrations of life, there are somber rituals of death, and in many parts of the Basque Country it is still generally the custom for a widow to wear black for the rest of her life. Though rare now, an early custom required children of the deceased to wear black for a year, and then, for *media luto* or the second year, the children were allowed to add some white to their attire. A death is announced in the little villages by the ringing of the church bells. Teresa del Valle (lecture, 17 July 1990) described a custom practiced in some Spanish-Basque villages of placing crosses made of black cloth on a deceased person's beehives as a sign of mourning. She also said that it is still common to go to the stables or barns to tell the animals of their owner's death so that the animals are prepared for their new keepers.

Roslyn Frank's article "The Religious Role of Women in the Basque Culture" informs us that women parishioners were responsible for the spiritual well-being of the members of their households both living and dead. In the church floor, representing each family in the village, were *yarlekuak* (flat stones), under which deceased members of each household were buried. It was the *serora's* (woman serving in the church) responsibility to receive bread and candles brought to the church by women as offerings in behalf of the souls of their dead ancestors. The candles were often placed on the family stone, or *yarleku*. At times of death, it was the *serora* and other female members of the parish who took care of the funeral rituals. The role of the *serora* in today's Basque Catholic churches in the old country has been devalued, but the strong sense of responsibility assumed by the women concerning the church and their family members, both living and dead, has not (1977, 153). Attending mass regularly to be instructed through the homily and to partake of the wine and wafer of communion are weekly rituals for most of these households.

Another whole body of lore surrounds the *baserriak*, or farmsteads, that dot the landscape of the Basque Country. The farmsteads defined roots and identity in another way. The homes were named, and the family living there was known by the name of the house. The *baserriak* of the Basque countryside are usually sturdy white stucco buildings with red tile roofs in a pastoral setting of rich farmland and rolling hills. The houses themselves have histories which often wind back through many centuries. Isabel Jausoro, born of immigrant parents and now a resident of Boise, Idaho, described part of her husband's ancient familial homestead which has been in the family for fourteen generations. "It has walls at least twelve inches thick, and the inside keeping place for the animals is still used and is kept immaculate;

the kitchen, after being remodeled, is more modern than my own!" I asked if there were any smell of animals in the house. She stated firmly, "No. It is clean. And that is all there is to it" (interview, 22 June 1993).

A typical arrangement of the traditional Basque *baserri* included indoor living quarters for the farm animals. The stable was on the ground level, but its ceiling, the floor of the family living quarters on the next level up, did not cover it completely. One end was left open. The third or top level, again with an open side, was usually an attic, or *gambara*, where grain, vegetables, and other food stuffs were stored. It was an efficient arrangement—both the animals and the people kept dry and warm—but it was potentially dangerous because of the opening at each level from which one could look down, or fall down, into the stable.

There are ancient traditions tied to the protection the house offers its inhabitants. For instance, a woman, after giving birth, was to remain under the protection of the roof of the house for forty days. She would not be considered clean until the priest gave her a special blessing. In order to go to the yard to gather vegetables or put out laundry, the woman would tie a house tile to her head in order to remain safe. Another tradition, no longer practiced, was burying an unbaptized stillborn child under the overhanging roof of the house. It was thought that the house, a sacred place, would protect the soul of the child. There were precepts attached to the houses and properties regarding boundary markers (which were to be respected) and the fireplace as the heart of the home where fire was considered a sacred, purifying element. It was at the table in front of the hearth where stories, legends, language, and the rosary were shared. There were even ritual blessings for the family dog to prevent it from running away! Though many of the old traditions have been forgotten, some remain strong. Since the fifteenth century, the house has usually been passed down to the oldest child, or oldest remaining child. The one who inherits the *baserriak* remains to run the farm and siblings have the right to return to the homestead for visits or permanently, as they wish.

Maria Rosa Hauser, (interview, 16 June 1993), described life on her family's farmstead as difficult but still the life her parents preferred. Many of the old farm houses have been modernized, but Maria's parents have kept their *baserri* the same way it has been for generations. They continue to live there, and they still run their small farm. A few years ago, her mother fell from the main level to the stable and broke her arm. Though she received immediate medical aid, the arm was permanently damaged, and it has seriously complicated the arduous lifestyle she and her husband still maintain in the countryside of Vizcaya. Maria has encouraged her parents to retire, but they prefer to continue working as long as they are able. This attitude is typically Basque. Hard work, no matter what the vocation or profession, has been a cultural expectation.

Traditional Female Occupations in the Homeland

Though there were exceptions, the majority of the women interviewed for this work had familial roots in the Vizcayan region of Spain. Most were American-born first-generation daughters of immigrant parents. The old country context that many of their mothers emerged from during approximately 1900–1925 was one of budding coastal industrialization and grinding rural poverty. The central Spanish government, the economy, and Basque nationalistic fervor were in turmoil, and the alternative for many Basques at that time was emigration to North America. Overall, most of the immigrants came from rural areas where women shared responsibilities with men but in different spheres. Most women could see no promising economic future for themselves. The men performed in the public sphere, and the women did their duties in the private atmosphere of the home and the church and, weekly, in the marketplace.

Like many older, traditional, European cultures, the Basques have a recognized patriarchal tradition in the public sphere. Roy Morrison mentioned Gustav Henningsen's fascinating work, *The Witches' Advocate: Basque Witchcraft and the Spanish Inquisition (1609–1614)* in his (Morrison's) text on the Mondragon cooperative in the Basque Country. Morrison wrote: "There is a long record of the imposition of patriarchal patterns and power in the Basque Country, including the repression of women as 'witches' and their resistance during the Inquisition" (1991, 144). On the other hand, and at a much later date before and during the Spanish Civil War in the 1930s, Basque women entered the public sphere in open protests of oppression.

Anthropologist William A. Douglass states that "egalitarianism between the sexes ... is but one manifestation of the complementarity of role playing that is characteristic" domestically (1969, 203). Another anthropologist, Sandra Ott, in her study of the rural French Basque village of Sainte-Engrâce, clearly delineates divisions of labor by sex, but states, in agreement with Douglass "a relative equality exists between the sexes which contrasts with reports for other European and Mediterranean societies where there is a marked subordination of women to men" (1981, 1993, 53). In a rural community with few outside political interests except among a small number of the young, unmarried people, the hard-working men and women of Sainte-Engrâce are self-sufficient and reasonably content with their style of life. Ott also notes that this equality is common in other parts of the Basque Country. Referring to male and female heads of the household as *bardin-bardina*, "equal-equal," she further states that "Extreme submissiveness in either sex is deplored for it allows one sex to dominate the other" (1981, 54).

In interviews I conducted for this work, I learned that when they were teenagers, many of the Basque women had been trained to be seamstresses. Housekeeping and domestic cooking were two other occupations mentioned frequently. Concerning occupations outside of the home, Teresa del Valle remarked: "In the Basque culture, the idea of women working is new. That is unlike the American culture where women have worked and [have been] models [for the younger generation] for many years" (lecture, 23 June 1990). The Basque women, del Valle said, are "just now beginning to gain 'power' in our society" (lecture, 11 July 1990). She defined power as the capacity to "exert decision-making in relation to persons, situations, things, and the distribution of resources" not only in a private domain but also the public sphere. Based on studies conducted in the Basque provinces, del Valle stated that the great majority of Basque women define themselves by the following in order of declining importance: "good mother, cleanly person, and hard worker." She further stated that the roles and behavior of women are still very prescribed, and in fact, most women still define themselves by judging how well they measure up to those "socially constructed norms" (lecture, 11 July 1990).

As early as the 1950s, industrial cooperatives were being formed in the Basque area of Mondragon. They were founded primarily by men; "single women could work, but married women could not be cooperators until 1971" (Morrison 1991, 147). Christine Clamp noted in her doctoral dissertation that in the early 1980s, women in Spain were underrepresented in the Association of Women's Commissions (organized by women in the cooperatives). Clamp argued that "women have yet to overcome the social and organizational barriers which keep them in the nonprofessional positions and underrepresented in decision making bodies" (1986, 192; qtd. in Morrison 1991, 147).

Roy Morrison, an American ecologist and energy conservationist, has presented further views of the public sphere and behavior of the Old World Basque women. In his study of the Mondragon cooperative movement for economic and social ecology in the Basque region of Spain, Morrison wrote a passage describing "Women and the Mondragon System":

> The women's movement, the end of Francoism, the
> surprising resurgence and durability of Spanish liberal
> democracy, and the increasing integration of Spain

into the European community have all led to a dra-
matic change in the position of women. The overt—at
times almost semifeudal—air of repression I observed
in 1965 and 1969 had changed dramatically by the late
1980s. There are abundant political graffiti, posters and
wall paintings in the Basque country, including clear
signs of feminist agitation—Aborto Si! (Abortion
Yes!) was popular on walls, and can accompany
OTANA fuera! (NATO Get Out!)—together with
startling color posters promoting a *korrika* (race) to
benefit Basque nationalist efforts. In Mondragon in
1985 it was reported that local women, after town officials remained adamant in refusing to accede to their
demand for easy availability of contraceptive devices,
threw chairs through the windows of the room as they
left a meeting. (1991, 145)

Ott describes the woman's role as one of strength that is
limited, by choice, primarily to the domestic sphere; del Valle
suggests a contemporary struggle by women to emerge from a private domain and gain empowerment in the public arena; and
Morrison describes women who have empowered themselves in
the public arena and are demonstrating their strength and
demands publicly and vigorously. For another generation, physical strength and endurance determined the lifestyle.

Lucy Arrien Echegaray, who came to the United States
with her sister Cecelia in 1942 and now resides in Elko, Nevada,
described her parents' farmstead near Rigoitia as a ranch. She
stated flatly (interview, 17 June 1993): "There was no chance
there. Only work." Lucy remembers herself as a small child carrying wood and water to help her mother. Typical of rural Basques,
her family went to the market weekly and sold vegetables, eggs,
and sometimes beans in order to buy sugar, coffee, and other
necessities. Now and then, Lucy said with an impish twinkle, one
of the children would snitch an egg. Though she felt her parents

suffered by having to work so hard because of poverty, the large family of children (seven boys and seven girls) was never hungry. "There was plenty of milk and plenty of beans. We also had corn-bread, and sometimes our mother bought little wheat breads. Each year one beef and one pork was killed, and they always made good *chorizos* (Basque sausages)." Lucy resides comfortably in Nevada now, but over fifty years ago, she and her sister choose to make the long, arduous ocean voyage to begin a new, uncharted life in the American West.

Women's Emigration to America

During the late nineteenth and twentieth centuries, many Basque women obviously chose not to remain in the narrow and restricted worlds that may have been designated for them. The selection process, concerning who would go to America and who would not, was complex and diverse. There are three general settings in the Basque Country: rural, coastal, and urban. The circumstances under which people left each area were different, but all had one common denominator, a need to economically survive. William A. Douglass quotes a poignant suggestion representative of many parents left behind, that the young often had little choice in their decision to leave:

> I know that when they grow up my children will leave me. I bear them no grudge since they would be foolish to remain here. I would leave myself but all I know is farming. I am what I am. I only hope that when I am old my children will send me money to hire labor to cut ferns each year. If they do so, I can carry on here until my death. (1976, 72)

Douglass points out, significantly, that the speaker was one of the most successful farmers in the village. (1976, 62).

The following pages describe the diverse circumstances under which four women left their Basque homeland and removed permanently to the western United States.

Cecelia A. A. Jouglard

Nearly ninety years old now, Cecelia is a beautiful Basque woman who came to America in 1942 from Guernica, Spain. She and her sister, Lucy, survived the horrific bombing of Guernica; the house in which they were staying, that of another sister, was completely destroyed (interview, 16 November, 1989). She recalls running wildly through the streets amid bodies and burning buildings. She was semi-hysterical because of the noise and heat, and, reaching the river, she threw herself in and fortunately was fished out by friendly Spanish soldiers. In her panic, she had forgotten that she didn't know how to swim. The soldiers laughed at her and teased her about trying to commit suicide. She said she knew it probably looked that way, but that really was not the truth.

Cecelia and Lucy and their twelve siblings grew up in a *baserri* (farmstead) in the countryside of Vizcaya and learned at a very young age to work hard. Her father died when Cecelia was five years old, and her mother died when Cecelia was twelve. The farm burned, and relatives helped the children still living at home. One of Cecelia's older sisters and her husband owned a fine restaurant, Restaurante Arana in Guernica, and welcomed both Cecelia and Lucy there. The older sister, Fernanda, trained them both to cook well and serve graciously. Though the restaurant was destroyed in the 1937 bombing, it was rebuilt and achieved a four-star rating; Cecelia became and remains a Basque-style gourmet cook.

In 1942, while still working for their sister, the girls had an opportunity to migrate to America. American military officers who frequented the restaurant helped make arrangements with the consul, and the two sisters traveled by ship to Cuba where an older brother met them. They stayed a brief time, and then traveled, again by boat, to New York City. Cecelia stated that she did not feel afraid, but that she was very sick during the entire ocean voyage.

In New York, they were met by Valentin Aguirre, a name well known and fondly remembered by many Basque immigrants of that general period. Aguirre, or people working for him, greeted Basque immigrants upon their arrival and welcomed them to America. Such brokers were common among immigrants of most nationalities. Cecelia has shared many of her engaging stories, and they will be found throughout this text.

Resu Goldaraz Goldaraz

A remarkable woman with unusual stamina and confidence, Basque American Resu Goldaraz was born in Yraizoz, Spain, in the province of Navarra. Her husband, Antonio, was born near Yraizoz. The term "remarkable" is appropriate because since her husband's death in 1978, Resu has been the successful boss-lady of an extensive sheep operation (interview, 12 November 1989). That is unusual for a Basque American woman. Sheep ranching is a competitive business run almost entirely by men. That part of her story will be told later.

After working for an uncle in Evanston, Wyoming, and saving some money, Antonio decided to establish a home in America. He also decided that he wanted a Basque wife. So, he returned to Navarra, met and married Resu, and then escorted his new wife to Salt Lake City, Utah. Resu's maiden name was Goldaraz, and her husband's was spelled the same way; however, it is generally the custom for Basque women to keep their own family names after marriage.

Resu has many relatives in the old country, and she has traveled there as often as her business will permit. Relatives there have often invited her to move back permanently, but her children have established themselves in America, and she would not go alone. Her life in America has been difficult since her husband's death, but less so than it would have been if she had not married and come here. She was trained to be a seamstress in

Navarra. If she had not come to America, she probably would have spent her life in or near her natal village as a farmer's wife. One of her brothers runs the family *baserri* now. He farms and also has a small dairy business.

Mary Louise Inda

Like Resu, Mary Louise states that she would either be the wife of a farmer or, perhaps, the wife of an industrial worker if she had remained in her native province of Vizcaya (interview, 10 June 1993). Mary Louise reports that her father and brother still run the ancient family *baserri*, and they also have a small dairy business. Her mother had determined that Mary Louise would be a seamstress and saw to it that she was trained by the best teacher in a nearby village. When her mother died while Mary Louise was still a teenager, the responsibility for the younger children as well as for assisting on the farm fell to her. Mary Louise does not feel that this was particularly unjust, but it was difficult, nevertheless.

In 1964, an uncle and aunt living in Reno invited Mary Louise to come to America and live with them. They said that she could take her time in learning English and that eventually she could train for a vocation or profession. Confident that she should not pass by this opportunity by, Mary Louise quickly made arrangements and, in fact, arrived in Reno before her letter informing her aunt and uncle of her imminent arrival. Lacking English language, Mary Louise hailed a cab and handed the driver the address on a piece of paper. Remembering the appearance of the house from a photograph, she went to the door after midnight and was greeted by a groggy but welcoming uncle.

When Mary Louise left for the United States, her grandfather was living with the family. A quiet but verbally supportive old gentleman, he hugged Mary Louise the day of her departure and said he was sure he would never see her again. Mary Louise assured him that she would be back often for visits. "But," she laments, "sadly, he was right. It was a few years before I could go back because I married in America and could not afford the trip for a while. He died before my first return trip."

Maria Rosa Hauser

Mary Louise Inda escorted me from Reno, Nevada, to Sacramento, California, in order to introduce me to Maria Rosa Hauser (interview, 16 June 1993), her dear friend and former schoolmate in the school for seamstresses in Vizcaya, Spain. (The name is a pseudonym. Maria's husband gave permission to tell her story but requested that their correct names not be mentioned.) "It is best, I think," Mary Louise suggested in her excellent English, "if I get Maria to tell you her story herself. She speaks a rapid mixture of English, Basque, and Spanish, so I will act as your interpreter if you need me."

As we drove around a bend in the highway, Mary Louise pointed out some massive bluffs in the distance. "Do you see those bluffs, Jackie? They belong to the Hauser family. Well, maybe not all of them, but I think they own about half of them." Soon we turned onto a very long driveway leading to a beautifully appointed, old Mexican-style *hacienda*. I noticed a large street sign on the left of the drive printed in black and white which appeared official. When I read it, I could hardly believe what I was seeing. It said, "SLOW DOWN MARIA." Mary Louise was smiling and said that Maria's husband had that made as a little, unsubtle reminder concerning his wife's driving style.

Maria greeted us warmly and took us to her immaculate kitchen. We were seated around a table, treated to icy beverages, and then got right down to business with the interview. Another Maria, a mutual friend of Mary Louise and Maria Rosa, and a fellow student in the village sewing school, was invited to the Hauser ranch many years ago by her father. He was a sheepherder for the Hausers, and he learned that the family wanted a housemaid. Recognizing an opportunity for his daughter, he sent passage money to her and helped her adjust to her new home.

Some time after Maria's departure, Maria Rosa received a letter from her stating that the Hauser family had two nice, unattached sons. Maria had made her choice and wondered if Maria Rosa would like to correspond with the other brother. She agreed to correspond, and soon she and her future husband traded photographs. After a while, Robert Hauser invited Maria Rosa to travel to the ranch for a visit. When she went to the consul to make arrangements, her visa was firmly denied. The consulate had heard about the correspondence, and thought that she would stay in America illegally if allowed to immigrate.

Maria Rosa wrote and informed Robert what had happened. Then she continued her very unpleasant occupation as housekeeper and cook for the demanding mistress of the sewing school. One day, as she was sewing, some boys ran in and told her that there was a tall, thin American in town looking for her. She did not believe them at first, but they finally convinced her. She walked out of the house, and there was the tall, thin American man that the village boys assured her was there.

Within six weeks, Robert had been baptized as a Roman Catholic by the village priest (his parents were Catholic, but he had never been baptized), banns were posted, and they were married in a traditional Catholic service in the little village church. Maria Rosa had her gown made in Bilbao and tells of a harrowing trip in a violent storm the day before the wedding when she drove to pick up her dress. Upon her return, she found that the bridge to her village had washed out because of flash flooding. She had to drive a long way around to the next village in order to get home. Furthermore, the day of the wedding, electrical power failed in the village, and her hairdresser had to help Maria Rosa carefully dry her hair in a wood-heated oven. She was late for her wedding, but it was successful, and she is now a proud Basque American wife and mother with a kind husband, two beautiful daughters, and one grandson.

The emigrant stories are various and abound among the older women of the culture. Almost always, as stated before, they were influenced by a hope of attaining a more promising life. Some young women in the 1930s and 1940s traveled to Mexico before eventually heading for work in one of the western states. I was told one fantastic story about a petite mid-twenty-year-old crossing the Mexican border under the hood of a Ford. She had been wrapped like a cocoon and was not under there very long. However, in her state of nerves and fright, she got the giggles and the border patrol officer thought he heard something. Her uncle's car was detained long enough for the officer to check the trunk and underneath the car, and then it was waved through.

In the early part of this century, young women and men traveled to America on ships under mostly uncomfortable conditions, endured the ordeal of immigration inspection at Ellis Island, and then often received a friendly greeting from Valentin Aguirre, the previously mentioned Basque hotel keeper in New York City. Aguirre made them at home in his Basque establishment, allowed several days of rest, and then arranged for their trip across the country to their new homes in the West (Douglass and Bilbao 1975, 375).

In the rural Basque Country, primogeniture is the tradition of inheritance. Whether the oldest child is male or female, that child has the first option to inherit the family *baserri*. Though the tradition is not followed as strictly or as often as it was in past centuries, many families still honor it. I interviewed one Basque American family in the West who has recently followed a form of this tradition. In their case, the oldest daughter inherited the family ranch. There was no family argument about the arrangement. According to tradition, any unmarried sibling may remain in the home for a lifetime, if he or she desires. Because many sons and daughters did not inherit property, they often sought alternative occupations and lifestyles. Some found and married people who had inherited a family homestead, although these marriages were not usually pre-arranged by parents. Because of the devout Roman Catholicism of the people, many Basque youths became priests or nuns. Some entered the professions, but most entered the growing industrial economy emerging along the north coast of Spain. Many others found their way to the American West and an entirely new way of life, establishing new occupational traditions.

This chapter began with Virginia Argoitia's story about the chair her grandfather made for generations of the family to use. For Virginia, the chair aroused feelings of comfort and belonging—almost familiarity. The next chapter's discussion of boarding houses, hotels, and homes established by Basques in the American West illustrates, in part, how the Basque American people continued familiar elements of their homeland. A discussion of sheepmen's wives and families illustrates how they have worked side-by-side to build a secure future in the United States. As the century and generations of Basques have moved on, more and more Basque American women have found professions and occupations outside of the home. The chapter will close with a discussion of their modern occupations.

2

A Real Home Smells
Like Garlic and Onions

Lucille Orriaga Ghiglieri and Irene Orriaga Arbeloa, sisters,
grew up in a Basque hotel on Douglas Alley in Reno, Nevada. Life on
Douglas Alley, which ran behind one of the hotels owned by their par-
ents, was an interesting adventure for Lucille and Irene. Vice, secret
meetings, honky tonk sounds, and constant comings and goings in the
alley held endless fascination. It seemed like everyone knew each other
and there were swing doors that never closed. During the hot weather,
Lucille and Irene slept outside on a sleeping porch, but the thought of
any danger never occurred to either of them. Life in the hotel on the
alley was familiar, fun, and always interesting. Lucille said that when
they were growing up, being Basque was something you just did not
talk about. Ethnicity was not an issue. Living in the hotel and having
family spread through separate rooms on the second floor seemed dif-
ferent, but at the same time better, than the American girls' homes.
When the sisters were teens, they began to attend club meetings in
their school friends' typical American homes. Irene thought their
homes were too antiseptic. "A real home smells like garlic and onion.
That is a home."

Boarding Houses and Bootlegging

Basque boarding houses, rooming houses, and hotels were numerous in the American West for nearly 150 years. The first living accommodations of this type in North America were probably established in California to serve fortune-seeking Argentinean Basques who arrived from the South American pampas region during the gold rush (Douglass and Bilbao 1975, 151–60). Other Basques came from the old country to seek their fortunes. As the unsteady search for gold turned into agricultural, cattle, and eventually sheepherding occupations, the needs of the slowly gathering Basque American society changed. As the sheepherding industry developed, Basque hotels and boarding houses were established in most of the western states. There was a need for Basque-speaking domestics to help operate these cultural havens for Basque sheepherders, and so, the women began to arrive from the old country. Close sisters such as Cecelia Jouglard and Lucy Echegaray were in their early thirties when they arrived in Shoshone, Idaho, where another sister met them. They both spent a few years working in Basque American boarding houses.

Most Basque women were in their mid to late twenties, or early thirties, when they made the ocean crossing. Before long, the strictly run hotels and boarding houses were nicknamed "marriage mills," for it was there that many lonely sheepherders met their brides and eventually established homes and ranches of their own. Besides possibly meeting one's life companion, the hotels provided many amenities for the single Basque herders: a link to the American community because the Basque proprietor could speak English, familiar Old World food and customs, a simple but clean room, a place to receive mail, a place to be nurtured if injured or ill, a place to store one's gear when away for seasons at a time, and most important of all, a place to speak the language and share cultural security and familiarity (Osa 1989, 317–23).

Presently, very few of these boarding houses exist outside of California. The few operations remaining are primarily now public restaurants such as the Sante Fe in Reno, Nevada, and the Overland in Gardnerville, Nevada. Jerònima Echeverria reports that of "the 119 Basque hotels and boarding houses that have been part of California's history, eleven still function in some capacity ... at Fresno, Los Banos, Bakersfield, Chino, and San Francisco" (1989, 235–38).

These early rooming establishments were often run by Basque immigrant couples who deliberately maintained a home-like atmosphere within them. There was often a *pelota* (hand-ball) court outside of the home where the men exercised and sometimes competed with one another. The hotels or boarding houses assisted Basque men in their adjustment to living in the United States and served as root, in a sense, to the formation of the Basque American culture known today. The hotels provided a community, and often families who did not live nearby visited and took meals there on the weekends. Some Basque men never learned the English language because they planned to return to the old country after accumulating savings. For these men, the hotel was a center for survival. The women's presence was important in the cultural shaping and even survival of the early Basque American society.

Preceding a discussion of Gracianna (Grace) Elizale, Lyda Esain, and Juanita Bastanchury, Etcheverria wrote, "My point is that Basque women had a much greater role in the survival of the early Basque communities than our literature suggests" (Etcheverria 1991, 4). In another work she noted that Basque hotels and the hotel network run by women were critical factors in the newcomer's transition to America. A woman hotel keeper's responses to human needs ranged from "buying a large burial plot in the local cemetery for bachelor herders, [to] tending to the needs of infirm boarders ... special care or bathing ... [or even] raising funds for one of her serving girls who was expecting her first child" (Etcheverria 1988, 6–7). Further, she stated, the hotel keepers gave more than most people realize. They gave

> more than working long hours in an endless work-
> week, more even than offering invaluable support to
> their husbands as business partners ... [They] extended
> themselves to their Basque counterparts and made life
> easier for those around them. Each became "the one"
> that Basque men and women would go to first for help
> in troubled times. In a sense they became trusted advi-
> sors to the Basque community. In addition, local
> policemen, lawyers, politicians, and other non-Basques
> seeking information or advice on Basque-related issues
> leaned to consult these "Basque senior stateswomen"
> before making bold decisions. (Etcheverria 1991, 8)

During the 1940s and 1950s, Louise Etcheverry, now of Rupert and Lava Hot Springs, Idaho, almost singlehandedly oper-ated boarding houses much like those of the last century. Born of immigrant parents in Mackay, Idaho, and married in the late 1930s to an emigrant French Basque who came to America in 1929 to herd sheep, Louise and her husband bought their first boarding house during the late 1940s in Pocatello, Idaho. They owned it for eight years. Later, they sold the Pocatello house and purchased another in Rupert, Idaho. Louise raised her two chil-dren and ran the boarding house alone while her husband estab-lished their sheep business (interview, 9 November 1993). Louise says Basque boarding houses and rooming houses were inter-changeable terms, "although there was more difference between a boarding house and what was called a Basque hotel, and that was that non-Basques, tourists and the like, could stay at the hotels. The boarding houses were usually run like homes for the herders and Basque men in other occupations, and only Basques stayed there." She never had any trouble in either of her boarding houses, even though, in addition to her family, she housed as

Louise Etcheverry, Rupert, Idaho 1996.

many as eight herders at a time. If anyone even looked like they might cause trouble, all she had to say was "There's the door."

Louise did all of the cooking, and she served three substantial meals a day. "No sandwiches," she states proudly, "only full meals," She also did all of the other housework, only allowing herself the privilege of sending the men's bed and bath linens out to a professional laundry. She made the beds each morning and, considering herself a quasi-bootlegger, sold drinks to the men in the evening if they wanted a mixed drink or some wine. Louise states that she bought the liquor legally but sold it by the drink, illegally. "The police knew what I was doing, but they never bothered me with it." In the evening at Louise's, many boarders played *muz*, a traditional Basque card game, and instead of money they often bet cups of *cafe royale*, a potent mix of coffee and Harvey's Bristol Cream. Some played the jukebox in the living room and just listened or occasionally asked Louise to dance.

In many hotels and boarding houses, in addition to the usual domestic chores, the young women were frequently expected to dance with the men on the long weekend evenings. Many boarding houses or hotels, like Louise's, had a pay bar and a jukebox to provide diversion and entertainment. A family atmosphere usually prevailed during the evening and during special holiday celebrations in both the boarding houses and hotels.

During earlier years, those of prohibition and the depression of the thirties, bootlegging by owners of Basque hotels and rooming houses became a risky but common and necessary custom. As in most European cultures, a Basque mid-day meal or evening dinner is not considered complete without wine. One of the Basque American women I talked to in Sparks, Nevada, related a story about two uncles and one aunt who were arrested and temporarily jailed on bootlegging charges during the 1930s. The "Prohibs" fortunately overlooked this woman's mother who was reluctantly involved. A child at the time of the arrests, my informant was determined to visit her family at the jail to see what it was all about. After a few hours, she returned to her mother's home proudly sporting ink-stained fingers. The police, humoring her, took her fingerprints, let her see her aunt and uncles briefly, and then sent her home.

Robert Laxalt's semi-autobiographical novel, The Basque Hotel, realistically describes Basque hotel owners' experiences with the "Prohibs." Laxalt relates a childhood memory of Pete, his protagonist, convalescing in a room next to the family kitchen and overhearing his father angrily lift a Prohib and set him on a warm but not scorching wood-burning stove. The Prohib left and did not come back (1989, 59).

Julie Gogenola Pagoaga told (interview, 21 June 1993) of a strategy her immigrant mother devised to import illegal liquor into Idaho from Utah during the late twenties and early thirties. Mrs. Gogenola, a woman her daughters called a master moneymaker, ran a laundry business in her home, and many of her best customers asked if she could get bourbon for them. Though her sheepherding husband accused her of being "bird-brained," she removed the back seat of her car and replaced it with a long, hollow box. Covering it with blankets, pillows, and most importantly, a "sick" child, she was never searched at the state border, though she was stopped many times.

Julie's mother later had a boarding house for herders and ran it primarily with the help of her daughters. Occasionally a girl from the Basque Country was hired. There were strict rules of behavior between the girls and the men. The girls worked long hours cleaning, changing beds, assisting with the cooking, and doing dishes. They did not eat with the men but rather ate later with the cook, in this case, Mrs. Gogenola. The girls were not allowed to drink or to single-date the boarders, although they were allowed to date in groups. Jerònima Echeverria quotes an early resident of Los Angeles on the life of a Basque hotel maid, "women who worked the hotels there were virtually slaves, performing the large variety of tasks needed to keep the enterprise going. Daily work hours began around six in the morning and lasted until the last customers were served, with breaks and/or free afternoon granted during occasional lulls in the hotels routine." (1989, 309).

In small boarding houses, most of the cooking, bookkeeping, errand running, and grocery shopping for the boarders, girls, and the family was done by the wife of the owner (Pagoaga interview, 9 November 1993). Often the husbands were sheepherders or cattle ranchers as well, and they were away at least part of the time. Though it was traditional for men to serve the liquor in the evenings, sometimes the husband/partner simply was not there. Louise felt uncomfortable about serving drinks when her husband was away, but fortunately he was usually there. Running a hotel or boarding house was an arduous occupation, and several women recalled their mothers falling asleep in the late evening still fully dressed. Though the business provided a livelihood for many couples, it was often used as an investment toward other occupations, primarily sheepherding or ranching.

Many Basque Americans, both male and female, continued to accrue real estate and have built substantial fortunes through property ownership. For many young women, the boarding houses or hotels provided a beginning, their stepping stone into a new country that seemed to have endless promising possibilities.

Cecelia Arrien Jouglard of Rupert, Idaho, and her sister, Lucy Echegaray, of Elko, Nevada, arrived in Shoshone, Idaho, after a train trip that seemed interminable. Cecelia (interview, 18 November 1989) and Lucy (interview, 17 June 1993) recalled passing through Chicago and imagining that Shoshone would be another substantially developed city. Their destiny was determined because their older sister had married and settled not far from Shoshone. When the train arrived at the small depot, the young women refused to disembark. The town seemed non-existent. From the train window all they could see was an expanse of brown soil and sagebrush, no buildings. The girls remained adamant about refusing to get off of the train and repeated, "No Shoshone. No Shoshone." Eventually they recognized their sister Juanita and her husband on the train station platform, and the conductor shoved them off of the train. The four traveled to Castleford, Idaho, about ten miles from Shoshone, where both young women were put to work immediately in their sister's home; Juanita and her husband had a sheep business.

The girls adapted quickly to the work, but in a short while, Cecelia became very unhappy (conversation, 22 June 1993). She wanted to work in a boarding house. Another brother, Salvadore, lived in Twin Falls, Idaho, and invited Cecelia to join him there. Cecelia went, and later Lucy joined them. Eventually Salvadore found work for both sisters in rooming houses. Lucy moved to Salt Lake City, eventually met and married a sheepherder from Elko, and, now widowed, lives there near her son. Cecelia went to work in a rooming house in Nampa, Idaho, which was owned by the Jausoro family. She later worked for a boarding house in Hailey, Idaho, and it was there that she met and married Prudencio Aldana, a Basque from

Vizcaya. He had come to America to herd, but when they met he was working in the Triumph Coal Mine in Hailey. The couple lived in Hailey for five years, and then they moved to Shoshone, where they owned and operated a boarding house of their own for one year. After that, they moved to Rupert to run a boarding house there, but Prudencio died a few months later. Cecelia was left alone with two young daughters to raise.

Another family named Inchausti settled in Hailey, Idaho, and owned and operated a Basque rooming house which gained a regional reputation for its outstanding Basque cooking. Visits from well-known celebrities taking holidays in Sun Valley were an occasional reward for the long hours Mrs. Epifania Lamiquis Inchausti, the heart of the establishment, spent in the kitchen. Dorothy Inchausti Ansotegui shared information (interview, 23 June 1993) about her mother, who was the happy and enthusiastic cook and manager of the boarding house. Dorothy's father was a foreman for the Drake Sheep Company in Challis until 1929. After that, he operated the Gem Bar, which was connected to the kitchen, dining room, and family living quarters. In the boarding house were six long-term male boarders who, because of their constant presence, to Dorothy seemed more like uncles than boarders. The family lived in a house and served the meals there, but the boarders lived in a separate building. Mrs. Inchausti was a private, shy person and conducted her home and the boarding operation in a quiet manner. She did all of the cooking and hired Basque girls to do the housework, help serve the meals, and wash dishes. Though she owned one Spanish cookbook which she referred to for desserts, her six daughters are not sure how she learned to make so many complicated meals and homemade breads. A few of her specialties were clams and rice, codfish (*bacalao y tomato*), pig's feet or tripe in a tomato-pepper sauce, squid in an ink sauce (*chipirones en su tinta*), red beans, and homemade *chorizos* or Basque sausage.

One evening during the mid 1940s, Clark Gable and a glamourous date made arrangements to eat at the Inchausti boarding house. They were accompanied by Bing Crosby and Gary Cooper. As it happened, when the celebrities' spokesperson called to make the dinner reservation, Mrs. Inchausti was gone on a very rare visit to Salt Lake City. Fortunately Tío (Uncle) José, a bachelor who knew how to cook, was there and the daughters convinced him that he could prepare a nice dinner. Though nervous, he served a dinner of meatless Basque spaghetti with a side-dish of lamb. Clark Gable's date was a particular fascination for Dorothy and her sisters, young teenagers at the time, because she was wearing tight slacks and high heels. Her outfit was quite a contrast from their mother's modest house dresses. Dorothy added further that the favorite of the evening was Cooper, who was friendly and who laughed easily. He also wore a memorable bright red tie. Crosby, she said, was very quiet and less friendly. Since these were such famous people, the young sisters quickly spread the word by telephone, and it seemed the whole town turned out for autographs.

Though their mother missed cooking for those celebrities, she had a cooking experience later that Dorothy reports more than made up for it (letter, 23 September 1993). When Sun Valley became a popular place for stars, Mrs. Inchausti got to cook what she called a "special" dinner. (Special meant she fed the boarders, family, and regulars and then cooked a complete meal for a later setting.) This meal was for Colonel Sanders of Kentucky Fried Chicken. She was shy, so she usually did not talk to the guests. She asked her daughters and some of the ladies of the community to serve the food. Amazingly to her, the Colonel entered her kitchen and told her: "Don't spread it around, but I think your fried chicken is as good as mine!" It was his way of thanking her, and Mrs. Inchausti never forgot it. She was "thrilled" to have him compare hers to his nationally known chicken. Her life in America was a life of hard labor, but her daughters remember her as happy and contented working, cooking, and operating her boarding house well into the sixties.

A Basque Hotel Family in Reno

Lucille Orriaga Ghiglieri and Irene Orriaga Arbeloa, Basque American sisters born in the 1920s, grew up in Basque hotels in Reno, Nevada, and shared stories about those years in an interview with Mateo and Gretchen Osa (15 May 1984). Their father had come to the United States in 1907, to Wellington, Nevada, where his brother worked on a sheep ranch, and their mother came in 1916 to Oakland, California, to work in her aunt and uncle's laundry. Their parents met around 1920 at a Basque dance in San Francisco. They soon married, and the girls were both born in Nevada. After a period of time working sheep, their parents decided to try the hotel business. They eventually owned several in Reno, including the Español, which was on Plaza Street across from Pacific Meat Market, and the Toscano, on Lake Street. They bought the old Santa Fe Hotel and moved there in 1936.

Life for their mother, the "business-head" of the family, was an endless round of work. Lucille and Irene wrote to me (letter, 23 and 24 August 1993) and shared some of their memories of their mother. When the girls were very young, there was an eighteen-year-old from France who helped their mother in the hotel, but for the most part, Mrs. Orriaga did all of the work herself. Their mother was intelligent and organized, and their father always asked and received her opinions before making any decisions. She seemed to be a mother figure to many of the Basque women in the community. She often visited with her sister and close friends on the telephone, and she enjoyed playing cards such as *muz*, *pedro*, and *solo*. Card playing was especially relaxing for her. She was a good listener and a trusted advisor, and many people went to her for counsel. She always cooked three meals daily, made appointments for the boarder's trips to the doctors and dentists, took care of the sick, and prepared special diets for boarders if necessary. According to these two daughters, she believed in God, honesty, and cleanliness, and she firmly instilled those values in her family.

The hotels their parents ran were as homelike as they could be made, and the two parents worked as a team. Mr. Orriaga did the banking and was sort of the public-relations man. He made himself available to interpret for the Basque boarders when they went to the bank, doctors, dentists, or stores. The couple openly participated in bootlegging, selling shots for twenty-five cents.

The sisters knew of at least one hotel (not Basque) that was used as a brothel or "red light" house during the war. It was on East 2nd Street and was a successful enterprise. The owner once remarked that she was in a business that made real money: "After all, those rooms could be rented out two or three times a night." In Nevada, it was not uncommon for Basque families who lived out of town to send their daughters to town to live in a relative's hotel in order to attend business school. Aware that an uninformed young female relative lived at the just mentioned hotel but did not know anything about the night activities, the sisters laughed when their business school teacher warned their class, including the innocent cousin, which neighborhoods they should avoid in Reno. Those very neighborhoods were where these three girls lived and happily called home.

Both women recall many changes after World War II. The gambling houses in Reno started serving food, sheepherding diminished, and many men moved into town and took apartments instead of staying in the Basque hotels. Some took other jobs and did not return to herding. Reno was growing and changing. There were many suicides among the working herders who didn't move into town because of the loneliness and isolation of being in the mountains for long periods of time with no human contact. The Basque hotels, boarding houses, and the occupations of the women who either ran them or worked in them also began to change. Daughters were sent to college or business school, and the era of the Basque hotels as homes, where men sometimes came in their youth and stayed until they were old, began to close.

Sheepmen's Wives and Daughters

In the United States, Basque emigrants often, but not always, settled regionally according to which side of the old country frontier was home. Many of the early French Basque and Navarrese settlements were made in southern California and parts of western Nevada. The largest groups of Spanish Basques formed settlements later in the nineteenth century in northern Nevada, southern Idaho, and eastern Oregon. Scattered settlements in Montana, Wyoming, Colorado, Arizona, and New Mexico were mostly of French Basque origin. Though regional differences among the Basques in America are played down more than they once were, it is still not unusual for individuals to identify themselves as either French Basques or Spanish Basques.

Though some Basque men returned to the old country in hopes of finding a bride, it is equally true that many marriages were the result of introductions in the hotels or boarding houses. Often individuals from the same provinces met and married, and sometimes the couples were from neighboring towns though they had never met in the old country. Sometimes the couple put money aside together to send home to the old country to enable their families to remodel and refurbish the old *baserriak* (farmsteads). They also frequently furnished young Basque relatives, male and female, with their first passage to America. Douglass and Bilbao state that these Old World kinship and regional ties are examples of "chain migration" (1975, 335), that is, by word-of-mouth or by kinship ties, one person helps another, and tells another, and the chain of migration continues through verbal links.

Thousands of men and women came to the United States to work with the thought of returning someday to the old country. Tree carvings in groves of aspen throughout the hills of

Aspen tree carvings on the Jouglard-Dredge Ranch, Caribou County, Idaho.

western America attest to the frequent presence of herders from the Basque provinces and to their loneliness for the outside world and their women. These simple carvings depict names of Basque provinces, dates, initials, hands, airplanes, and, often, hearts and designs. Alicia Dredge's son, Frank, a Basque American teenager who offered to take me horseback riding in the aspen groves above his parents' ranch, pointed out several carvings and found one with initials and a date of 1937 that was distorted but still clearly legible.

The Basque sheepherders, in the last century and in this one, gained and maintained a good reputation based on their skill and dependability with the animals, and their willingness to spend long periods of time alone in the hills. In spite of the belief that they were all sheepherders in the old country, it is closer to the truth to state that some learned sheepherding in the old country, some learned either in Argentina or Uruguay, and most learned in the hills and plains of the western United States. Though many saved their money and returned to the old country permanently, others eventually built their own large bands of sheep here and became operators instead of herders. Their women were usually at home taking care of the house and the family.

After marriage, Basque women often stayed at home and raised the children, but that was not usually all that was expected of a young wife. Many women became directly involved in the sheep business, the rooming house or hotel business, or both. Virginia Argoitia, of Sparks, Nevada, shared her mother's favorite personal narrative about her first cooking experience in an isolated sheep camp (interview, 8 June 1993). A young mother of two, it was her responsibility to prepare the meals for her family and several herders and to keep the camp in order while the men were out with the sheep. Beans are a staple part of the camp diet, but this young immigrant woman had never prepared them. First she started a fire and set up the pot. Not knowing that the beans would swell and seem to multiply as they cooked, she put far too many into the bean pot. After a few hours, beans began to spill out into the fire. She dished some out, but they just kept swelling and spilling over.

Finally, in desperation, she dug a very deep hole and began scooping the extra beans into it. She was afraid to be caught wasting food, in part because of the Basque cultural tendency to be frugal and in part because her husband had firmly warned her that they must be very careful with the food. She respected his instructions; after all, they were very far from the nearest town and additional supplies. Eventually she got the beans buried and the burial plot disguised. She then went on and prepared the rest of the meal.

In the Basque sheep camp, Virginia said, it is a tradition to feed the dogs after the people. The husband, his men, and his dogs returned that evening and the men set about eating their dinner. One of the dogs, Bolo by name, began to sniff and furiously paw the earth where the beans were buried. Virginia's mother chased him off and scolded him, but he kept returning to the spot and repeating his enthusiastic yipping and scratching. Finally, Virginia's father got his gun and stated his intention to put the dog out of its misery, assuming it had become rabid. Virginia's mother confessed quickly because that particular dog was the children's pet. A good laugh was shared by everyone, and the young mother was forgiven. In spite of the isolation and heavy work of feeding so many in addition to caring for young children in the wilderness, Virginia said that her mother remembered the times in the sheep camp as the best years of her life.

Louise Savala Etcheverry, now past eighty and still working with her husband, Jean Pierre, in their large Idaho sheep operation, continues to contribute to the business as a shopper, runner, and sometimes cook for the men of their outfit. Though the business is run mainly by their son Henry, Louise and Jean are always there to take care of the workers, the lambs, and to perform whatever other work that needs to be done. A French Basque, Jean Pierre still practices the most stringent measures to protect each lamb and ewe from unnecessary death. When a ewe

Sheep camps at the Etcheverry Ranch, Rupert, Idaho, ready for the coming season on the range.

dies giving birth, Jean Pierre covers her living lamb with skin from another ewe's stillborn. He nestles the living lamb, wrapped in the dead lamb's skin, close to the ewe who lost the lamb. The two usually bond quickly, and that way, a minimum of animals are lost. Louise is always close by with hot coffee, wholesome food, or a helping hand for husband and son and their workmen, no matter what the season.

Cecelia Jouglard shared (interview, 16 November 1989) what her working life had been like from the 1950s to the late 1970s. With her second husband, Frank, she helped run their large sheep holding operation. Part of her responsibility was to go with him to the isolated camps, almost daily, to see the herders and keep them furnished with fresh food and news of the outside world. Cecelia shared some of the experiences she had with herders who had come from the rural hills of the old country and who sometimes did not know American foods. One year, over a period of several months, Cecelia noted that the herders were requesting an extraordinary amount of jam. She furnished it without asking any questions, but her curiosity finally took over. What she learned was unusual, but, she remarked, "It was typical of bored people." It seemed that several of the men were eating jam straight from the jar, thinking it was some kind of sweet dessert. They had not seen bottled jam in the rural Basque Country in the 1960s, and mistook the sweet mixture as a marvelous American dessert. Cecelia explained to the men how the jam was intended to be used, and they cut back accordingly.

"Now and then," Cecelia continued, "there are men who eat so much it is hard to believe. They are never fat, to the contrary, they were often very thin." One day, Cecelia went to one of the camps and noticed that the herder had prepared a large steak and a full dozen eggs to be eaten. She asked if he were expecting some company, and he assured her that he was not, he was simply hungry and preparing a meal for himself.

Cecelia said that there was almost always at least one herder in their troup of employees who seemed to excel in making sheepherder's bread. A large golden round, the bread was traditionally baked in a cast-iron Dutch oven that had been buried under the earth in a bed of hot coals. The bread produced was large and high, and it had an almost cake-like texture. According to Cecelia, this style of baking was learned in the Americas and it was virtually unknown in the Basque Country except through word of mouth from those who had visited America. She once joked with a good bread-making herder that when they both got old they should go to Vizcaya and open a bakery to produce sheepherder's bread. She thought the enterprise might have been successful, but the herder died.

Alicia Aldana Dredge is Cecelia's oldest daughter. Alicia has a master's degree in Spanish and has studied in both the United States and in the Basque Country. Her younger sister, Elene, also has a master's and studied both in the United States and southern France. Alicia remarked that having been sought out for this study was significant to her because she was just recognizing that Basques, along with other American ethnic groups, had become 'important' to America in a larger sense in the latter half of this century. She remarked that as a child she had been called "a dirty Basco" by misinformed Anglo schoolmates in central Idaho. "Time changes attitudes" she remarked. She added that she was relieved that social attitudes were changing for the sake of her son. Her words were significant. By the very act of the interview, a serious contextual grounding was established which many women welcomed. It affirmed and validated life efforts which most of these women perceive as extremely important (interview, 12 October 1989).

Alicia recalled that her mother's home was very much like Spanish-Basque homes which she observed in the Basque Country during her university years. Basque or Spanish was often spoken, and the foods and decor were European. When the child Alicia left for public school in the morning each day, it was as though she was literally stepping out of Europe and into America. Upon her return from school, the process was reversed. "It was a good way to grow up," she says. "I always knew more than one world, but I didn't feel any conflict" (interview, 12 October 1989).

An irony of tradition is represented by the responsibilities of these two well-educated young women. When Frank Jouglard, Cecelia's second husband, died, it was necessary to determine how the large sheep and ranching business would be run. Thousands of sheep as well as thousands of acres of land were at issue, and careful planning was needed. The older daughter had little interest in the operation of the ranch. The younger enjoyed working the ranch, riding fence, working with the animals, and the changing seasons of the sheep operation. Because of their mother's strong Old World tradition of primogeniture, the responsibility of managing and operating the ranch and sheep business fell to the oldest daughter, Alicia. Her American husband is a rancher, so she shares her responsibilities with him. The younger daughter, Elene, left the area of the ranch altogether and now works as a successful office manager for a utility company in an Idaho city. Both daughters are remarkably amiable about the arrangement, though they perceive the arrangement differently. Alicia thought the responsibility of the ranch fell to her simply because, after marriage, she remained in the same region; Elene perceives primogeniture as the reason the estate was settled the way it was. Alicia remarked (interview, 28 October 1989), "Well, you do what you have to do." Alicia's son has shown some interest in and aptitude for the sheep ranch, but the sheep industry is rapidly changing and, as Alicia explained, "Soon, a future as a western rancher and sheep operator may no longer be as reasonable an option for a life work choice as it has been in the past. Further, competition from New Zealand and Argentina has changed the American wool market. Some American sheep operators have been forced to leave the business."

Denise Bengochea is a Basque American teacher, recently married, who I met in the Basque Country. She is the proud granddaughter of Concepcion Bengochea, who was born in Spain in the Basque Country on 25 April 1907 (unpublished first-person narrative, 1986). The mother of two children, Concepcion and her husband worked for Catherine and John Etchart, Montana ranchers, for many years. She moved to their ranch at Tampico, Montana, when she was expecting her first child, primarily because Tampico was close to a town. After the birth of the baby, Mary Theresa, she went to the home ranch, which was about fifty miles from Glasgow, Montana. A year later, in 1935, a boy, Mitchel, was born.

The ranch had a rock house, "the best in the country because it was made old-country style with rocks and with a nice basement for storage. The potatoes did not freeze." The babies stayed healthy, and Concepcion cooked. The following is a partial account of her responsibilities:

> I made lots of chili con carne. They [the herders] filled up with that. The first thing I cooked for Mr. Etchart and Mitch Oxarart was beef tongue in the sheep

camp. They had butchered a beef two days before, and it was ready for cooking. This was not new to me because in Spain we did not waste anything.

The time went by … then [1939] I went to Tampico to do the cooking for Mrs. Etchart because Mary Theresa and Mitchel were getting ready for school.… I cooked for their family, the workmen, the teacher, my kids and visitors along with cleaning the milk cans and separator, making butter and canning all of the fruits and vegetables in half gallon jars. This was an all-summer job besides cooking and doing all of the dishes. On Thanksgiving, lots of company came and I served big dinners.… Friends from Glasgow came for Christmas too, and I prepared them complete Christmas dinners. Mrs. Etchart had a small elevator to send the food upstairs from the kitchen to the dining room when they had company. The rest of the time everyone ate in the kitchen downstairs, visitors and all.… When I cooked for shearers in the camp … there were over 25 people to cook for and I even made bread for them. (Bengochea 1986)

The work Mrs. Bengochea performed would seem familiar to many of the women discussed in this work.

I visited with a mother and two teenaged daughters who live far from a Basque cultural center in a rural area of Idaho. The daughters' paternal grandfather came to America in 1929 from the province of Labourd, France, to herd sheep. He eventually married a Vizcayan woman born in the United States. The girls' grandfather and father speak, in addition to English, Basque, Spanish, and French fluently. The girls' mother is not Basque. I asked the girls if they were interested in their Basque heritage in spite of the fact that, due to distance, they could not be active in a dancing group or attend any kind of Basque club meetings. They laughed and the older one replied: "We are Basques. That is just the way it is and it doesn't matter where we live. We go to several festivals each year, and we both like the foods. Our father is a sheepman, and his heritage is ours. Even if we don't speak the language like him, we know a lot of Basque words and phrases." The younger of the two girls was working on a paper for her high school honors history class. Her subject was her grandfather's immigration experience, including the entry process at Ellis Island in New York, and his crossing of the United States without the advantage of English. The paper described her grandfather's first experiences as a young, isolated sheepherder on a desolate hill in Ely, Nevada, just a few weeks after his arrival in America. The young sheepherder eventually built his own business, which is now managed by his son, the girls' father (Etcheverry, K., N., and D., interview, 10 April 1995).

Modern Occupations of Basque American Women

In the American West, there are very few sheep operations now relative to how many there were even twenty-five years ago. Like other Americans, the Basques are establishing themselves in professions and occupations often far different from the traditional rural occupations of the first Basque immigrants. However, there are still many women who are proud to be engaged in assisting their husbands in the traditional sheep industry (or participating fully themselves as Resu Goldaraz of Soda Springs and Rupert, Idaho, is), and these women consider themselves and their occupations very modern. Louise Etcheverry, for instance, though past eighty as stated above, still carefully looks after the various needs of the herders her husband now imports from Chile and Peru to work in his large Idaho sheep operation. In her words: "Of course I work. Who else is going to do it? I've worked all my life, so why should it be any different now?"

In a personal interview (8 October 1989) Louise explained that her work continues to include taking sojourner workers to the immigration offices when necessary, seeing to their medical needs, ordering and picking up food and supplies, registering cars and trucks used in the operation, making sure there is a good cook for the workers during lambing and shearing, and other assignments.

The Basque women of the American West are ethnic by choice. They carry no visible physiological marker of their ancient Iberian heritage. The Basque physical appearance is European, and coloring ranges from a fair, almost Scandinavian, look to deep olive-colored skin and dark hair. Among my informants were several redheads with clear, green eyes, and also women with light brown hair and the fair skin of the British Isles. Many choose to study their Basque roots, and many seem not to be interested. Several young women participate as counselors in summer camps for Basque American children, and still others devotedly practice and perform in the Basque dance clubs throughout the United States. Though not important to all of them, for many the Basque identity generally remains an important ingredient of their self-concept in an America that continues to note and expect cultural diversity. They may look and act just like any other Euroamericans, but they share more than a collective consciousness. They share Basque blood. In the next chapter, their voices will reveal what that means to them and to the rest of us.

The daughters and the granddaughters of the women discussed above as well as other women interviewed or studied for this text followed a wide variety of non-professional and professional occupations in the United States; they were teachers, professional interior decorators, landladies, dancing instructors, anthropologists, medical technicians, nurses, professors, newspaper reporters, writers, hairdressers, department or drug store clerks, certified public accountants, engineers, working partners in sheep operations, waitresses, university professors, or librarians. A clipping from an Idaho Falls newspaper describes a "petite Basque dynamo named Espe Alegria...[who] has packed her life with activity from serving as a Spanish interpreter for the courts to a long stint as the only disc jockey in the United States whose program was in the unique Basque language" (*The Post-Register* 12 October 1989, B-7). Basque American women have become involved in many activities and professions. The Basque identity, though no longer as relevant in the everyday lives of some Basque American women, is still of continuing importance in other ways.

One young third-generation Basque American woman, Christine Landa, since married to an Italian American, is a certified public accountant in San Francisco:

> I have little time to go to the Basque Cultural Center now, but when I first moved to San Francisco from Idaho and didn't know anyone, I went a lot. I am not looking for a husband at this point, but I know that when I marry, I will raise my children with a knowledge of their Basque heritage. It is really important to me. My brother and I are hoping to make our second trip to the Basque Country in the next few years. (interview, 4 July 1993)

Monique Laxalt Urza, mother, lawyer, and fiction writer, "one who wears many hats," as she put it (interview, 15 June 1993), has published her first book, *The Deep Blue Memory*. Semi-autobiographical, it is a story mingled with haunting imagery and almost tangible impressions of the ancient homeland with its "deep beneath," and of the new, gleaming American West of "dust ... sage ... pine ... and the deep blue lake" (1993, 59–61). Laxalt-Urza's book gives profound and insightful expression to being Basque in America.

Some Basque American women have followed traditional paths as homemakers and assistants to their husbands in spite of advanced education. As noted, Alicia Dredge has a master's degree in language studies but helps her husband run their sheep and cattle operations. She also spent many years volunteering a few days a week in the office at a her son's school when he was younger. Some full-time homemakers have used their extra time to help create new interpretations of being Basque in the United States; examples of those women's efforts in invention and maintenance of ethnic traditions will be discussed below.

Angeles Arrien, who has a Ph.D. and is a member of the Cecelia Arrien Jouglard family, is an anthropologist, educator, and corporate consultant. She codesigned and implemented the Social and Cultural Anthropology Program at the California Institute for Integral Studies and authored the spiritual perspectives module for the external degree program at the Institute of Transpersonal Psychology. She is a core faculty member at both of the above institutions and is also on the faculty of Antioch University and John F. Kennedy University.

Jerònima Echeverria, Ph.D., is a professor of history at the University of California in Fresno, and her research on Basque hotels in California has greatly enhanced the understanding of Basque American women's contributions to the Basque culture. Many young Basque American women are studying their history and culture at universities in Reno and Boise as well as in the homeland. There arc more Basque and Basque American women with academic degrees now than ever before, and their research and writing will add significant information to the record and preservation of their culture.

3

Mountains Don't Move,
But People Do

Julie Gogenola Pagoaga, who lives in Shoshone, Idaho, far from her grandchildren, imports them from her different married children each summer with many purposes in mind. First of all, she wants the cousins to know each other, and for them to know her. Next, she hopes to instill in each of them a fond sense of their Basque heritage. Perhaps most of all, she wants to place in their minds memories of the high country where their grandfather and their great-grandfather once tended sheep and where their great-grandmother ran a first-class boarding house. They speak Basque words, sing old songs from the homeland, prepare ethnic foods, and generally have a few weeks of fun with a Basque flavor. Julie, who enjoys a widespread reputation as one who knows her culture among her family, friends, and neighbors, mentioned that she had added saffron to lasagna to give it a more interesting, "sort of Basque," flavor. Julie is a consummate tradition inventor and bearer.

Inventions and Syncretisms

Basque Americans have been constant about maintaining various traditions from the old country since their arrival in the United States; however, over the first several decades that constancy was not perceived as a conscious effort at cultural maintenance. The Basque rooming houses and hotels served a very real need, particularly for the men and women who did not speak English. The language, foods, games, entertainments, shared interests and memories, and other cultural symbols practiced there, in a natural way, had no overlay of deliberate invention and syncretism. Today, however, to maintain Old World culture among an ethnic group that is scattered across America and no longer shares a common occupation and common tongue, the group must plan their cultural survival. Basque Americans appear to be successful in doing that, and the women, like Julie Gogenola Pagoaga, play a constant and deliberate role in the effort.

Identity survives through maintenance, invention, and a legacy of pride. In "Defining Identity through Folklore," Alan Dundes reminds us that "Folklore is clearly one of the most important, perhaps *the* most important, sources for the articulation and perpetuation of a group's symbols" (1989, 8). Continual festivals and celebrations, traditional foods and lore, collective memories, and, for many Basques, preserved and cherished language provide stable connections to a cultural center, even when someone feels a little decentered. A sustained identity often means having the courage to change things, knowing old wood must be treated occasionally with new oil and someone is always inventing a better way to do it. To keep what is original means doing more than encapsulating tradition; it means using the tradition dynamically.

The past, real or invented, imposes fixed or formalized practices (Hobsbawm and Ranger 1983, 2), and at several levels among the Basque Americans, the Catholic church provides a foundation and framework for such ritualization. Conservative religious traditions are embedded within the culture through ceremony and ritual and even manifest themselves in the ubiquitous bread and red wine at every mid-day and evening meal. At the same time, dynamic elements are present in adaptions to popular American society. Parochial school fundraisers, which feature Basque foods and music but include openly non-Basque clogging performances and auctions, are decidedly syncretic. When descriptive narratives emerge after events such as these, elements are selected and shaping or invention takes place. One might hear afterwards, "You bet. We had a great Basque dinner and school fundraiser at the Elk's Club last Saturday night. They served lamb and beans and we danced the *jota* afterwards. We sold sheepherder bread at the auction and one loaf went for $100.00. Nobody raises money for the school like the Basques!" (Louise Etcheverry interview, 6 April 1997). In this telling of the event, only the Basque elements are emphasized. Cultural codes and markers (food, dance, purpose) are transmitted, and the shaped narrative imparts an affirming ethnic identity in a world threatening to become a melting pot. Linda Dégh reminds us that "Storytellers in the same community constitute an intricate network" (1995, 8). Many of the stories and life experiences shared in the following pages interconnect and overlap.

Folklorist Barbara Kirshenblatt-Gimblett, wrote that "the immigrant experience, which so often involves culture shock, generates its own culture and folklore" (1986, 39). When Cecelia Jouglard and Lucy Echegaray talk about their refusal to leave the train in Shoshone, they are generating their own narratives—their own folklore which is repeated and circulated until it becomes a part of the new cultural collectivity. They are expressing their values and how they made the adjustment to what appeared to be a hostile and uninhabited landscape (particularly when Shoshone was compared with what they had seen of Chicago when their train passed through there on the way to the West). As Julie Pagoaga and others like her demonstrate, the

Children dancers trained by Lisa Corcostegui, at a Basque picnic in Reno, Nevada.

Basque women adjusted their traditions to the new world and created their own identity-maintaining narratives.

This first section of chapter three will look at some traditions and folklore of the Basque American people in the United States contrasted specifically with some of the Old World beliefs and practices discussed in chapter one. Invention and syncretism has taken place in order to ensure cultural survival of the Basque heritage for following generations of Basque Americans. Some traditions have been preserved intact and some have been adapted and even reinvented to suit various purposes, some have been newly invented, and some, as Father Garetea said about the Advent bread custom of the old country, have been entirely forgotten or abandoned.

As discussed in chapter one, curiosity about the origins of the Basque people continues to be a topic of conversation and even humorous conjectures in the United States as it was in the old country. A few years ago, I was invited to attend a Basque picnic in Reno, Nevada. I was honored by the invitation and was given an enameled pin to wear which had *Euskalerria* (historical and traditional name of the Basque Country) written on it. For that day I was an honorary Basque. The picnic was held at a park in Reno, and activities included a dance demonstration presented by children and youths, horseshoes, a few card games, and a traditional Basque dinner. It was a beautiful, sunny day, and men and women were visiting and having a friendly, wholesome party.

There have been very few uncomfortable moments in gathering the material for this study; however, at the Basque picnic, an unexpected moment revealed intriguing mores and attitudes of several Basque American women in Nevada. A verbally aggressive Basque American man approached me and said he was going to teach me an important point in Basque history. He said he would let me think about it a while, and then return to quiz me. He had been enjoying plenty of cool wine on a hot summer day, and I was surrounded by friendly Basque American women and felt quite safe, so I let him continue. He asked me if I knew the origin of the Basques. I said I had heard a few versions, but I had no idea what his story would be. He then leaned very close to my face and quietly said: "The Basques are the issue of a French whore and a Basque sailor. That's where they came from." He laughed and walked away.

I turned to the women who had been watching the exchange, but they had been unable to hear what he said to me. I inquired about him and was told that he was a retired teacher who was now working for the education system in another capacity. At that point they did not ask what he had said but assured me that he was quite a decent fellow. After a while, as promised, he returned and very formally, loud enough for all to hear, asked me to explain the origin of the Basques. I told him that I could not remember. He asked the question again and appeared to be agitated that I would not answer as he wished. Again, I pleaded forgetfulness. He swore and told me that he had heard I was a teacher, but he certainly did not know what kind. He returned later to replay the same scenario.

By this time, the women were curious to know what the exchange was about. I explained and said that I just did not want to repeat his origin thesis. The women agreed with my choice, proceeded to scowl him down, and he did not return to our table. Later the woman who had invited me to the picnic laughingly remarked that many of the Basque men felt their presence was a very special gift to the ladies. She added that the women were delighted with the way I had handled my interrogator. As people are sometimes defined by their opposition, this exchange revealed to me the bond the women share, in a sense, to protect themselves against possible misuse or even verbal abuse. By my responding in a way that met with their approval, it also created a new bond between them and me.

Less off-color origin stories told among Basque Americans are similar to those told in the old country. A frequent introductory version is that Basque was the original language of the Garden of Eden. I was told that, with wry smiles and a wink, several times in Idaho and Nevada. The joke about the devil not being able to influence the Basque people because of the difficulty of the language, the consequence being that the Basques are exceptionally good people, has also been told to me many times. With straight faces and a variety of styles, men and women never seem to tire of presenting the story for newcomers to the Basque American culture. There is always a laugh after this subtle reminder that the Basque ego is intact.

Because Basque studies and histories from the old country are translated into English both there and in the United States, ancient myths and folk tales are becoming more available to the American public. Examples include myths mentioned in chapter one extolling the mysterious cave goddess of strength called Mari. The figure Mari has been interpreted by a few scholars to represent one of Western Europe's earliest matriarchies.

That concept is strongly denied by other scholars. However, though the Mari figure is well known in the public sphere of the Old World, only a few of the Basque American women I interviewed were aware of this tradition.

In the Basque Country, all adult citizens are guaranteed political rights regardless of class, race, or gender, and the government is well aware it must honor social rights in the public and private sphere. As new generations of Basque women in the old country emerge from the home and join the public sphere in a vast range of professions and occupations, jokes about women's power ring hollow. In this day of long awaited equality for women, appeals for empowerment of both sexes reverberate throughout the Basque Country as they do around the entire world, but in actuality, though most Basque women are honored and treated well, some Basque women and Basque American women are still devalued within their own culture. Hence, among the Basque Americans at home and at gatherings in the United States, gentle allusions to the power of the Basque women continue.

My perception is that this construct is used light-heartedly and intended as a harmless affirmation of the women. However, when asked about the concept, many interviewees flatly stated that Basque American women were mentally and physically strong because of generations of very hard work. They bring this quality to bear by *willing* their heritage not to disappear under the countering strength and tempting process of American acculturation.

Some of the women are openly and energetically engaged in the process of negotiating a dynamic identity of survivals and inventions. As Janet Inda, of Reno, Nevada, stated concerning the women and their cultural contributions (telephone interview, 1 April 1995):

> We are working at it. We have established a Basque golf tournament at Gardnerville, Nevada. Golf is a part of today's American culture, and we want people

to do what they want to do, but with a cultural connection too. Not only that, there are golf courses
springing up all over the Basque Country now. You've
heard of José Maria Olazabal, of course. He is the role
model and hero of our young golfers.

I asked Janet just who was influencing whom as far as the
golf courses in the homeland. She laughed and said: "They are
copying us." The golf tournaments are an example of adaption
and invention. There are Basque golf tournaments now forming
in parts of California as well as Nevada. There are few golf
courses in the mountainous terrain of the old country. Yet, like
many Americans, young Basque American men and women
enjoy the game. For a people not afraid of establishing a new
interpretation of their Basque American identity and their sense
of exclusiveness, Basque golf tournaments were a logical choice.

Most of the immigrants came from rural areas where
women shared responsibilities with men, and assumed responsibilities in the church. The perception that women were the strength
of the home and responsible for the spiritual and physical welfare
of the family was often carried to the United States by these
immigrant women. In the summer of 1993, when I mentioned to
Carmelo Urza, a professor at the University of Nevada-Reno and
a Basque American born in the old country but raised in America,
that I was curious about the so-called power of the Basque women
and had heard it mentioned often, he leaned back in his chair and
laughed heartily. Then he leaned forward and said: "Jackie, you
will find no story in that. Everyone knows that the Basque women
rule. They have always been in charge." A few weeks later, 15
June 1993, I interviewed Monique Laxalt Urza, the lawyer and fiction author mentioned above, at the Urza home. Monique and I
were visiting and enjoying the last of a beautiful Reno evening in
their garden patio, when Carmelo emerged from the house. With
a friendly smile, he served an artfully arranged tray of iced beverages. Soon after, their oldest child asked permission for an outing

with friends. Carmelo and Monique conferred and jointly gave the boy permission. Their household and family appeared to be managed with cooperative authority.

On June 11, 1993, also in Reno, I tape recorded an interview with three American-born Basque women, Cassie Duarte, Benedicta Elorza, and Mary Cendagorta. Cassie Duarte said her mother had the strength of a survivor. Cassie's father died while the children were still young and left her mother financially unprepared to meet the needs of the family. Somehow, through community help, domestic work, and ranching, the family survived. As Cassie put it: "They worked hard there. They worked hard here. But here, it was better. Here there was a hope for a better future. There, there was nothing" (interview, 11 June 1993).

Mary Cendagorta said that when she was a child her parents retired from their labors in America and took their family to the Basque Country. She stayed there until she was twelve, and then she was returned to California to attend high school. While in northern Spain, Mary perceived that the males were often strong and patriarchal with the women. When I asked these women about the supposed mystique or power of the Basque women, they pondered momentarily and then Benedicta stated: "We women have as much power as we want in our homes. Our men have sort of become Americanized over here. They pretty much behave toward us like most American men behave towards their wives." When I asked for further clarification, she said that she felt that the men wanted wives who were clean and would work hard, but that the women could run their houses the way they wanted. Cassie indicated her agreement. Both of these women had worked along side of their husbands in various occupations, but they had both been the primary caretakers of their homes and, in each case, of their sons. Mary, whose deceased husband had been a pharmacist, said that her husband had always been fair to her and that she agreed with the others, but only to a point. She reaffirmed that she had observed patriarchal households, even abusive households, run firmly by Basque American men both in Reno and in the old country. She suggested that not all of the men seemed to be able to give up the domineering traditional style of many husbands in the Old World.

The strong Basque American identity, among both men and women, sometimes serves people from the old country who visit the American West. A frequent visitor from the old country, Santo Arrien, from the province of Guipúzcoa, told me that visiting Basques in the United States repeatedly reinforces his own sense of Basqueness (conversation, 15 June 1990). Arrien particularly enjoyed visiting the festivals called *Jaialdi*, a week-long celebration in honor of Basque Americans, held in Boise, Idaho, in 1987, 1990, and 1995. Idaho, reporting roughly 4,500 Basque Americans in the 1990 census, is the state with the highest population of Basques in North America. It was at *Jaialdi* in 1990 that I first heard the not uncommon declaration by visiting Basque performers that Idaho is the eighth province of the Basque Country. This honor was bestowed by the visiting *bertsolariak*, or improvisational poet-singers from the old country, who recognized the presence of hundreds of their former countrymen and countrywomen in the Boise audience.

Sisters Lucille Borda Rose and Marie Borda Swanson can remember singing in the style of the *bertsolariak*, or poet singers, at the table after big meals in their parents' hotel in Gardnerville, Nevada. These were made-up songs, they said, and verses were invented by individuals, usually men, who had just returned from visits to Spain and France. The sisters could not recall specific examples but said the verses were about the overseas trips, the old country, and, sometimes, political themes. These memories recalled a time during the thirties and forties when there were many Basque herders in the hotels of the West. The versification of the *bertsolariak*, an old country custom, was adapted for use at a Basque American table.

Another ancient symbol of the Basques, the war cry *irrintzi* described previously, is an eerie sound often heard during times of excitement when Basques are gathered. Under the right

A craft booth, *Jaialdi* 1990, Boise, Idaho.

Male dancers, *Jaialdi* 1990, Boise, Idaho.

circumstances, it can be heard far and wide. At the 1990 *Jaialdi* in Boise, teenagers and slightly older youths had climbed a stone wall and were standing on top practicing their versions of the cry just for fun. A sheepherder named Henry Etcheverry (interview, 15 November 1990) told me that the cry was often used in the mountains of America to let scattered herders know of one another's locations. Competitions for best *irrintzi* cries are popular at Basque festivals both here and abroad. Men and women compete with these seemingly inhuman sounds, and both genders win the contests. I observed an *irrintzi* competition at the 1993 Winnemucca Basque Festival in Nevada. A perfectly hideous war cry emitted from a fragile looking woman in her early twenties; she won the contest without any serious challenge. In the old country, the *irrintzi* was forbidden during the Franco years because the Spanish government saw it as a cry of rebellion. However, it is commonly heard at festivals and celebrations both there and here now.

In an interview in Reno, Nevada, 14 June 1990, Denise Inda described games that some young adult Basque Americans were designing to enable themselves to learn and subsequently test themselves about symbols of the Basques and elements of their language. Patterned after the style of the popular American game Trivial Pursuit, Denise said the game is popular among the youth and gaining popularity among older Basque Americans in Reno. She said that it is designed to be fun and educational, and that it is surprising to her that the young people really know so much about the ancient history and culture.

The old farmsteads of the rural Basque Country were mentioned in chapter one. In the interviews, almost every woman who had spent any time in the Basque Country mentioned the farmsteads of their extended families there. This was true of both the immigrant women who had been in this country for several decades and the middle-aged second and third generation Basque American women who had been born in this country and had only visited northern Spain or southern France. The knowledge of these old homesteads seemed to be more than just a random subject for discussion; idealized as the *baserriak* were in these discussions, they seemed to perform the role of an important insider topic. The memories of the farmsteads defined specific roots and identity. The *baserriak* were also mentioned by some of the younger women who had visited the homeland of their mothers and grandmothers for short periods of time or had studied or worked there for extended periods. Most of these women came from rural family roots, and nostalgia and appreciation for the beauty of the old ways has remained present in their collective memories.[6]

In many of the living rooms or dining rooms where the interviews were conducted, there were fine oil paintings or colored photographs of homes in the Basque countryside. Sometimes the pictures represented a husband's family homestead, sometimes a wife's, and often both. The paintings always included tidy white stucco buildings with red tile roofs in a pastoral setting of rich farmland and rolling hills. Without exception, the women proudly pointed out the depictions to me and shared memories of farm life and their time there as residents or visitors. The immigrant women described a life of hard work and shortages; the American-born visitors, many of them outsiders to the kind of life the immigrant women felt fortunate to escape, observed how beautiful and clean the *baserriak* were and how remarkable it was that some of them have been maintained by the same families for hundreds of years.

Marie Borda Swanson (interview, 30 June 1993) said that in the old country her mother's family home was in the town where her grandfather was the mayor. Her cousin's father still lived outside the town in an old-fashioned farmstead. According to Marie, when she and her sister Lucy visited, "The day we got there it smelled good, but boy, a couple of days later we went with them not knowing [we were coming] and—I don't know how they stood it!" (Meaning that because the animals lived in the house and the straw was soiled, the air in the *baserri* was not fresh.)

Lucy particularly enjoyed the peacefulness and tranquility she experienced there. She saw women working on the hills in dresses, with big aprons covering their skirts. I remarked that I had seen people dressed in the old ways, walking ox-drawn carts along the village roads in the Spanish-Basque region. Such an experience is like a time warp, and it surely reminds most contemporary people, Basque or otherwise, of an earlier, less complicated way of life. Nostalgia offers a safe, temporary escape to the imagined tranquility and tempo of another time in another world. In addition to reinforcing identity, the shared memories of the old farmsteads comfort and secure Basques who live in the accelerated lifestyle of the United States.

The fondest childhood memories of Maribelen Goldaraz Goodenough, called Mary, the daughter of Resu Goldaraz, are of several trips that she took with her mother and brother to see her maternal grandparents (interview, 12 February 1991). They owned and operated a large *baserri* in the province of Navarra. Her uncle, who also has a dairy operation in the nearby town, now owns it. Mary still enjoys her memories of orchards, gardens, cousins, swimming streams, *paella* (saffroned rice), and chocolate served with bread. For Mary, visits were a time of joy and laughter. She has not yet returned to the homestead as an adult but hopes soon to take her non-Basque husband to meet the cousins she has not seen since her early teens. Mary's memories of the old country are positive, but because she lives in the outskirts of a small town in Idaho and works full-time, she has no opportunity now to use the language, to mix with other Basque Americans, or even to cook Basque foods because of the difficulty she has obtaining authentic ingredients. However, if she has children, she says, "They will be raised Basque style."

Kirshenblatt-Gimblett has stated that "A community and its culture are defined as much by what is rejected as by what is accepted, by what is discarded as by what is retained" (1983, 42). The *baserriak* look charming, but depictions of them do not show the daily drudgery of survival in the rural Basque Country. Memories of farmsteads are diverse, but Basque Americans who did not live there for any length of time have romanticized them. The invented narratives of the Basque American storytellers, intentionally or unintentionally excluding particulars, shape perceptions of the *baserriak* for outsiders and inexperienced progeny.

Personal narratives often reveal the sense of identity, personal values, and ethical codes of the tellers. By repeatedly sharing stories of the *baserriak*, the Basque American women reinforced their own sense of identity as uniquely and positively Basque. They happily narrate their memories of them again and again at family and social gatherings and with interested visitors. Visits to the rural homeland, recalled through shared memories and stories, are valuable aspects of the Basque American's found and created American identity.

Oral Traditions

Folklorist Sandra Dolby-Stahl wrote that "The experiences at the base of personal narratives and the values that are expressed through them are original elements the tellers add to the tradition of the genre when they create their stories" (1989, 12). The Basque American women I interviewed told many stories about their own experiences and about their children's experiences as well. In many instances, as in other cultures, the children brought both positive and negative elements of "America" home, and the mothers had to sort out the children's experiences for them.

In the vernacular folklore of the Basque Americans, stories abound of ethnic slurs or *blason populaire*. One of the most common mentioned by the women I interviewed referred to being called black Bascos. The term is peculiar in that the Basques have typical European coloring and often have very fair skin and light brown or even reddish colored hair. One specula-tion is that the term originated with the dark tans the herders often had because of the outdoor work in the strong western sun. Sometimes Basques were perceived by the uninformed to be gypsies with strange and foreign beliefs. Because of the obscurity of their language, their natural clannishness, and their devout adherence to the Roman Catholic faith (an outsider religion in most of the western United States except among Hispanics), wild assumptions were made about their cultural practices. Because of these perceptions, many Basque parents ceased using the Basque language in their homes. They taught their children English as well as they could so they would not be handicapped or taunted at school. Cecelia Jouglard (interview, 15 June 1990) recalled a second grade teacher who asked her daughter Alicia if she spoke her "mother's dirty language." This was in the fifties in a small Idaho town. Cecelia went to the school and confronted the principal with the incident, but no apology was forthcoming.

Elene Aldana Robbins told me a story about her Basque language acquisition (interview, 14 June 1990). Alicia, the old-est daughter, spoke Basque fluently but this younger sister did not. Elene, frustrated by her mother's resistance to teaching her the language of their heritage, began to spend more and more time with some cousins who spoke Basque and wanted to learn to speak English. Elene and Alicia taught English to the cousins, but at the same time, Elene deliberately learned to speak Basque. One day, while Cecelia was braiding Elene's hair, Elene began to speak to her mother in fluent Basque. Cecelia was shocked and surprised but, as it turns out, altogether pleased that her daughter cared so much about the language. The mother and daughters still communicate in Basque when they are together.

The language may be valued now by many Basque Americans precisely because it was devalued in the past. Many American-born Basques avoided using the language because of incidents like the one described above; however, a few of the women I interviewed stated that they understood but now regretted their parents' choice not to teach them the language when they were children. The unique language remains a part of the heritage of the Basque Americans, but now that there are third and fourth generation progeny in the United States, use of the language is not common. Most of the young people speak English and study Spanish or French in school. Some take courses in Basque at the Basque Cultural Center in Boise or at the University of Nevada in Reno, and a few of the youth are able to go to the Basque Country to study.

Though language is an important binding element among Basques in the old country, there are other elements that keep the Basque Americans bound together as a community. Oral lore and customary superstitions are common in all cultures. Marginal distribution is a phenomenon that suggests that great distance from the cultural core usually strengthens folk custom and belief. Basques are not an exception to this phenomenon. Basque American women are generally spiritual and have well-defined traditional moral codes and strong family ties. On the other hand, their traditional proverbs, sayings, customs, and beliefs sometimes reflect pragmatic wisdom and a philosophic attitude toward codes, which are occasionally broken. One narrative shared with me (anonymous, interview, 14 June 1990) described a child born to a Basque American youth and an Anglo girl out of wedlock in the late sixties. The infant was adopted by an Idaho physician and his wife and never told of her origins except that she was adopted. The girl, inexplicably, was drawn to Basque studies after attending a Basque festival in Idaho and eventually learned of her biological roots by pressing her adoptive parents. She contacted her paternal grandmother who welcomed her into the clan, taught her about her heritage, and even sent her to the Basque Country to study the language and culture for a year. No condemnation was forthcoming for the son, the girl's biological father, or the circumstance. The grandmother said: "So, these things happen. She was connected to us and something inside of her told her that. Who is to question such things? Now she knows who she is."

As has been noted, Basque Americans can be clannish; they bonded tightly as non-English speaking strangers in a foreign land. When financially and emotionally threatened, they turned to jokes, quips, and common stories from the homeland to provide a familiar island of security. Bronislaw Malinowski stated that "Wherever there is danger, uncertainty, great incidence of chance and accident, even in entirely modern forms of enterprise, magic crops up" (1979, 40). Belief in magic and in a preservative faith are closely aligned. Pat Beiter, a retired professor of history from Boise State University, narrated the story of a young Basque emigrant warned by his mother "to be careful of his faith in that irreligious country."

> When he was on the train heading for Idaho he noticed many people's lips moving much like those of the women he had seen saying the Rosary in his own village church. He wrote his mother after arriving, saying she need not fear for her son's faith because many people on the train were praying. He later learned that these people were chewing gum, something he had neither seen nor heard of before. (n.d., 11)

Because of the network of boarding and rooming houses and because men and women often moved between them, many stories made the rounds. From Idaho to Oregon to California and back again, I heard many variants of the same stories. As mentioned above, one of the most repeated was the story of the devil and his attempt to tempt the Basques. An amusing variant of that story says that God promised the devil that he would have a chance to be delivered from hell if, after seven years, he could learn to speak Basque. The devil agreed and went down to earth to the Basque Country. After seven years he had only learned to say *bi* (yes) and *ez* (no). A huge storm came up, lightning struck, and the devil was thrown to the ground. When he got up, he realized that he had forgotten the two words that he had learned. He told God that he would rather go back to hell than spend another seven years trying to learn Basque. There is now a saying among the Basques that, because of the devil's frustrations with the language, Basque people cannot go to hell (Wasil 1970, 486).

Rita Wasil collected proverbs and superstitions from the Basques in Oregon for her master's thesis. The collection is housed at the University of Oregon Folklore Archives, and the following are a sampling of that lore:

> Its own nest is lovely to every bird.
> Basque women should not have their pictures taken during pregnancy; it damages the spirit of the baby.
> When ill, a Basque woman puts medication on the soles of her feet because nerve endings in the feet carry the solution to the rest of the body.
> The Basque house is always open to any of its children. All must share in its goods as well as in its labors.
> There is no small quantity that will not reach all; nor is there any large quantity that will not terminate.
> A home without a fire is a body without blood.
> The salesmen needs only one eye. But not even one hundred are enough for the buyer.
> As turbulent and muddy as his water is, never say, of it I shall not drink.
> Fish and guests spoil on the third day and must exit.
> While herding sheep, I give orders to my dog ... and he to his tail.
> A true Basque wears his beret even at meals. He removes it only in church, in bed, and sometimes when playing *pelota*.

Herders make thick bread in Dutch ovens on the range.
Always they scratch each loaf with the sign of the
cross before cutting the bread. (1970, 486–87)

These sayings were repeated most often by older members of the community, and were meant to convey wisdom and
humor. They were often passed down through families, and
repeated at what seemed to be appropriate times.

Louise Etcheverry, (interview, 12 February 1991) first
mentioned a variant of a Basque proverb which I have heard
her repeat many times. At a fiftieth wedding anniversary party
in 1991, Louise said she had commented: "The mountains cannot ever get together, but people will always get together," a
variant of the words used for the title of this chapter. Though
Louise could not recall where she first heard that old saying, it
again demonstrates identity reinforcement in its metaphorical
evocation of the ancient immovable mountains, the Pyrenees
frontier between Spain and France, an image extended now to
America.

Alicia Aldana Dredge (interview, 12 February 1991)
said that Spanish-Basque Catholics are generally superstitious.
When her mother, Cecelia A. A. Jouglard, was a young woman,
she often had dizzy spells. She believed that if she prayed to certain saints it would help her, and that is still her practice. Also,
Cecelia had a nephew who was slow of speech. The family
believed that if he went to a certain church in Rigoitia, in the
province of Vizcaya, and kissed a stone there, he would be
blessed with normal speech. Alicia's story ended there, so I
asked if they took him and if he was cured. Alicia gently said,
"Yes, he was cured."

Cecelia, in turn (interview, 12 February 1991) described
a folk belief based on an omen that she claims she and Alicia
have seen fulfilled many times. "If it is raining on the second day
of the month," Cecelia said, "it will rain all the rest of the
month. Further, whatever the weather is on the second, the same

type of weather will follow throughout the month." Both mother and daughter admonished me to watch that one for myself. It can be important for a people whose livelihood depends on the weather to be able to predict what is coming.

Rites of Passage

Though Basque American women are generally thoughtful and earnest about their Roman Catholic religion, their culture, like other cultures with roots in a distant past, has strands of folk belief that is still sometimes evident both in the United States and in the old country. The women practice many customs that they believe originated someplace in the Old World of their ancestors.

A selection of these begins with customs attached to birth and pregnancy. Jean Etcheverry Landa Chisholm and Alicia Dredge both described (interviews, 12 February 1991) a Basque belief they had heard many times concerning eating a loaf of bread. If the person eating it happens to be pregnant, the baby will be a boy. Virginia Argoita, of Sparks, Nevada (interview, 8 June 1993) remembers her Spanish-Basque mother often saying "Gold for the ears, good for the eyes." It is the custom among many Basque mothers to pierce a female child's ears with tiny gold earrings as soon as possible after birth. The earrings are usually left in place for many years. Alicia Dredge (interview, 18 February 1991) noted that Spanish Basques followed the custom common throughout Catholic Europe of naming a newborn baby after the saint on whose day the infant was born or baptized, though it is not as common as it was earlier in this century. Her mother, Cecelia, was born on November 21 and baptized on November 22, Saint Cecelia Day. Cecelia's sister, Lucia (Lucy), was born on December 23, Saint Lucia Day. In the past, children were baptized almost immediately after birth; now christening is delayed several weeks. It is not anything distinctively Basque that makes the naming custom significant but rather the association with Old World identity that a Basque American gives it.

Many first and second generation Basques in the United States have given their children typical North American names such as Denise, Christopher or Christine, and Bernard. Third generation Basques are beginning to reach back to traditional ethnic names, often of ancestors or of mythic Basque figures for their children. According to Lisa Tipton Corcostegui (interview, 15 June 1993) Aitor, one of the male children who performed in dances at the Basque Club during Reno's annual picnic in June 1993, was named for a mythic father figure in the Old World Basque tradition. Lisa added that she and her husband plan to give their future children typically Basque names. She mentioned a baby girl she knows who was recently named Ana Miren. Other popular girls' names Lisa listed are Argia, meaning "light," and Amaya or Amaia. This careful naming of children indicates an intensification of ethnic marking. Lisa, who works as a counselor in the yearly music camp held for Basque American children, said that at a recent Chino, California, camp, each child and counselor assumed a traditional Basque name. Name tags were necessary for the first few days, but as the names were learned, they became great sources of fun.

Naming demonstrates Basque American efforts to maintain visible and repeated reminders of their cultural heritage. I met a young Basque American elementary teacher, Denise Bengochea, while studying in San Sebastian, Spain, in 1990. The granddaughter of Concepcion Bengochea, recently deceased, Denise stated that her Basque surname was important to her sense of heritage and personal identity. As the granddaughter of Basque emigrants, she was raised in rural Montana, where her extended family still ranches. Denise visited relatives in the old country during that summer and has returned several times since. As Lisa and Denise demonstrate, the strong efforts of some Basque

American women to preserve their ethnicity include links to that ethnicity through personal names.

Basques celebrate birthdays much the same as other Americans. However, one old tradition that some practice is the gentle tugging of a child's ear once for each year. Alicia Dredge recalled (interview, 23 October 1989) an elderly Basque sheep-herder, employed by her and her husband on their sheep ranch in Idaho, who noticed a boy's decorated birthday cake on her kitchen table. He inquired how old her son Frankie was and then began to tug Frankie's ear. The boy did not understand at first, but after a reassuring nod from his mother, laughter ensued.

Because young Basque American children seldom hear the Basque language spoken, Basque words have been set to the familiar tune of "Happy Birthday" and have proven appealing to children. The song, "Zorionak" has been used to teach Basque American youngsters a few sounds and words of the Basque language:

> Zorionak zuri,
> Zorionak beti,
> Zorionak, zorionak (or name),
> Zorionak zuri.

> Congratulations to you,
> Congratulations to you,
> Congratulations, congratulations (or name),
> Congratulations to you.
> (Bilbao and Guerricabeitia 1987, n.p.)

Miren Rementeria Artiach is a Basque American mother who lives in Boise. She helped compile songs for a booklet in which "Zorionak" is printed. Miren told me (interview, 12 October 1991) that a familiar song included in the collection is "I Wish You," a Basque version of "We Wish You a Merry Christmas." The Basque and American versions are as follows:

Nai dot zuri Gabon onak
Nai dot zuri Gabon onak
Nai dot zuri Gabon onak
Eta urte barri.
Zorionak zuri ta zure sendiari
Nai dot zuri Gabon onak
Eta urte barri.

I wish you a Merry Christmas
I wish you a Merry Christmas
I wish you a Merry Christmas
And a Happy New year.
Greetings to you and to your family.
I wish you a Merry Christmas
And a Happy New Year.

These songs were not a part of the Basque culture in the old country. They have been recreated in Basque in order to provide young children the opportunity to master and enjoy some of the ancient language of their heritage. The hope of the teachers is that the children will become intrigued enough to learn more of the difficult Basque tongue.

Catholic Basque weddings in the United States follow few of the traditions of the old country. However, by reading popular books about Old World customs and by sharing what they learned, many Basque Americans are aware of what weddings were like in the past days of the rural Basque Country. They incorporate some of the traditions into their modern wedding celebrations. Louise Etcheverry told me about a Basque American wedding she had attended in Idaho (interview, 4 December 1993). Though the wedding itself was traditional and performed in the Catholic church, the reception had a few unusual components for a Basque American wedding. The music was not typically Basque, and the combo that played included a noisy electric guitar. The foods served did not include the traditional lamb.

Louise said it really was a beautiful wedding and that she recognized that times and traditions are changing. Louise's granddaughter was married in July 1997 in a traditional Catholic service which included mass. Her reception included a buffet with foods ranging from shrimp to lamb and vegetables. Wines and cake were served, and each guest received small gifts made by the bride. The music was a mixture of songs, American and Basque, and the lively Basque *jota* was enjoyed by the bride and groom and almost all of the wedding guests.

A non-Basque acquaintance, whose husband is a Basque sheepherder in a northwestern state and who has requested anonymity, laughingly shared a story about her wedding night. Her husband, self-designated "a wild and crazy Basque mountain man," was so exuberant about finding a good woman and getting married that at some undefined point in the night he threw his hands around her neck and "cut loose" with a loud, long, and screeching *irrintzi* cry of joy. She was frightened to tears, and he has never repeated himself (anonymous, interview, 16 March 1989). Though I have asked several Basque people if they have ever heard of the yell being used this way, I have been unable to determine that it is. However, judging from the energy and enthusiasm I have observed in Basque youths from Boise, Idaho, to Pamplona, Spain, and the many *irrintzi* cries I have heard, it would not be surprising. The cry is a popular noise of joy for those who know how to make the sound.

There are Old World customs practiced occasionally in the United States surrounding the remarriage of widowed people. Cecelia Jouglard explained (interview, 20 March 1990) that if a widow should remarry, as Cecelia did several years after the death of her first husband, the ceremony is often performed very quietly with little celebration. Cecelia and Frank Jouglard's marriage ceremony took place at five o'clock in the morning. They were attended by a few family members, the priest, and the altar boy.

In *The Long Journey*, a text about urban Basques in the San Francisco Bay region, Jean Francis Decroos writes about an "elderly woman who noted that her deceased son expressed the wish to have a Basque funeral and to be buried wearing the *beret*" (1983, 107). In 1990, when I was in a San Sebastian shop in order to purchase *berets* or *txapelas* for the men in my family, I was told that customarily in the Basque Country, the *beret* is only to be worn by men who have become secure financially but that tourists buy them without knowing the custom. I was assured, with a smile, that it was not required that I know the lore to make the purchase.

Basque American Festivals

Folk festivals, both in Europe and in the United States, are an important, almost ritualistic part of community life. Both commercial and nostalgic, Basque American festivals in the United States are frequent. Sarah Baker Monroe has pointed out that "These ethnic-conscious celebrations are becoming increasingly standardized" (1995, 100). There is a repetition of similar events from festival to festival every year. Young people at the Elko festival in July, 1993 complained that they were bored and loving it at the same time.

The "First National Basque Festival," the first truly organized western Basque festival, took place in Sparks, Nevada, on 6 and 7 June 1959 (Douglass 1980, 115–30). A Nevada gambling casino owner, though not a Basque, decided to sponsor the event as a commercial undertaking. His wife was a Basque American and so was his casino manager. The late fifties and sixties ethnic revivals in this country were welcomed by Basque Americans because though they had maintained small social pockets of their heritage here in America for decades, their Basque American culture was changing. The economy of the Basque Country had improved so there was less need for Basques to find work in the United States. The importance of Basque American hotels and rooming houses where the language was spoken, familiar cuisine was served, card games such as *mus* and

Maypole at the Elko, Nevada, Basque festival, July 4, 1993.

briska were played, and customary celebrations were organized and enjoyed, was waning. In the 1950s and 1960s, fewer Basques came to this country to stay, and fewer hotels and boarding houses remained in operation.

The ethnic revivals, which Basque Americans joined by enlarging organizations and celebrations already in place or establishing new ones, reinforced and strengthened fading traditions. The first organized festival was syncretic—a Basque festival which mixed Old World and New World Basque elements including testimonials, a sheepdog exhibition, a *muz* (card game) competition, folk-dance exhibitions, music, athletic contests, and a barbecue followed by a dance. These activities are still typical elements of the yearly Basque American festivals. The festivals serve as fixed events for preserving the continuity of the Basque culture in the West. The purposes of the Basque festivals both in Spain and in the western United States differ; those in the old country are often linked to the celebration of saints' days as compared with celebrations of ethnic survival in the U.S. Both, though, are largely participatory in the sense defined by John Moe. Moe describes a participatory festival as being made up of a largely homogenous population which takes place period-ically. Though Basque Americans invite the public to their cele-brations, the participants are mostly Basques who take part in the planning and playing out of the many regional festivals. The national *Jaialdi* festival, held in Boise every five years, is an exception in that more of the public attends, but it is participa-tory and still predominately Basque. Moe suggests that a semi-participatory festival is one with a clear distinction between participants and observers, such as a community fair. A non-par-ticipatory festival, he states, is one where a heterogenous popula-tion arrives on periodic dates to view a contrived situation such as a craft and demonstrations show (Moe 1977, 33–40).

As discussed earlier, Teresa del Valle has pointed out (lecture, 9 July 1990) that some intimations of rebellion against authority are often evident in the Basque festivals in the old country. In the playing out of aggression, described earlier, by the male youths toward girls and women, resentments and hostilities are openly demonstrated. I did not observe that kind of behavior in any of the Basque American festivals, perhaps because they are more structured.

The Basque *Jaialdi* '90 festival in Boise, Idaho, was quite a different kind of celebration from the Basque Country festival. There was a similar *Jaialdi* in Boise in 1995, and the Boise festival programs reflect very similar celebrations. The Boise festivals were a week long. They had food and souvenir booths and plenty of soda, wine, and beer. Like the festival in Spain, they were crowded with people of every age and featured parades, marching bands, and marching children. But there were a lot more differ-ences than similarities between the events.

Though there may have been incidents of rudeness and discourtesy to women during the *Jaialdi*, I did not observe any; neither did I observe anyone who was out of control because of drinking. The American festivals were orderly. The *Jaialdi* were highly organized and ran almost exactly on time. Activities ranged from a Basque Film Festival, which included important new films, to mid-week lectures by leading Basque studies figures and Basque government officials to a long Friday evening of Basque entertainment held at the Boise State University Morrison Center. On Saturday, the old Idaho State Penitentiary grounds were used for parades, booths, athletic competitions, musical performances, dancing demonstrations, visiting, and a multi-course Basque meal in the evening. On Sunday, a Basque-style mass was held at St. John's Cathedral in downtown Boise, and it included costumed Basque dancers. The mass was celebrated by a French Basque priest, and one of the highlights of the celebration in the church was the beautiful responsive singing, in Basque, between the priest and the congregation. The church service was further enhanced by a brief dance of celebration around the altar by the *Oinkari* dancers of Boise.

The European and American festivals serve different cultural purposes which is why there is so much difference between them. In the Basque Country, there are individuals who, though not openly engaged in resistance to the central government of Spain in Madrid, still harbor resentment and idealized perceptions of independence and a reinstatement of the ancient *fueros*. At times of celebration those feelings are sometimes released in relatively harmless activities. In the United States, on the other hand, the festivals are a public demonstration of successfully transplanted ethnic pride, integrated and functioning creatively within American society. The Basque American festivals serve also as reunions and renewals for the people and consistently display a positive interpretation of ethnic revival, syncretism, and invention.

Foods

Basque American women often use food as a nexus that connects identity-reinforcing social interactions and personal family relations. In many cultures, food serves as a collective communal marker, and the Basque culture is no exception. Conversations between group members evoke memories of shared moments and shared foods. Festival meals at Basque American celebrations in the West are delicious and very similar. They usually include lamb, beefsteak, beans, rice puddings, and wine. Similar also are food choices for meals served privately to guests. For instance, I was served *bacalao a la Bizcaya*, a salted cod served in a delicate tomato-pepper sauce, in private homes in Idaho, Nevada, and Spain. The repetition of favorite tastes and aromas, often including the homely garlic and onion, provides comfort and reinforces ethnic centering.

Lucy Echegaray (interview, 17 June 1993) said that a common saying in her home after a large meal is "We eat like a king if he eats like we do!" As mentioned earlier, Lucy and her sister Cecelia Jouglard were trained to cook in a fine restaurant owned by their older sister, Fernanda, in Guernica, Vizcaya. Following one of my interviews with Cecelia on 20 March 1990, a cold, blustery afternoon in Rupert, Idaho, I was invited to stay for dinner. I accepted the invitation and then was told that I could do nothing to help. Because my home was nearly one hundred miles from hers and I had hoped to drive through a formidable mountain pass in daylight, Cecelia invited me to rest a while and said that dinner would be ready promptly. She had prepared most of it ahead of time, and she served it in the mid-afternoon. The dining room table was set elegantly in an array of porcelain, crystal, silver, and linen. The dinner was a bright and beautiful seafood repast that featured *bacalao a la Bizcaya*, tossed lettuce salad with a simple oil and vinegar dressing, boiled green beans and potatoes, black olives, fresh bread and butter, red wine, and strawberries with cream. The cod, a favorite fish of the Basques and for centuries a staple food of northern Spain, had been purchased in dried form and had to be rehydrated by soaking it in running water for many hours. The tomato and pepper sauce was mild but flavorful.

Another dinner I had with Cecelia featured squid in ink sauce (*chipirones en su tinta*). Alicia, her daughter, teasingly stated, "The ink sauce will turn your mouth black." While I was in San Sebastian, Spain, I ordered *chipirones en su tinta* at a restaurant in the old part of town. It tasted exactly the same as that I had been served in Idaho. The squid dish is difficult to prepare and is only served on special occasions and at holiday time.

Also, while I was in the old country, I conducted several interviews with Felisa Echevarria, a Basque woman who had lived in Pocatello, Idaho, for many years while her husband worked for the railroad. After the third or fourth interview, Felisa invited me to stay for dinner, and I was amazed to be served almost exactly the same cod dinner I had enjoyed in Rupert. Even the salad dressing was identical. The only real difference was that in San Sebastian prior to the meal, Felisa served Dry Sack sherry, thin slices of goat cheese, and French bread.

Some of the women homemakers I interviewed said that their husbands preferred to eat only Basque-style cooking. However, most of the women prepare a variety of typical American foods and serve them alternately with Basque foods. Commonly served Basque foods include olives, vegetable soups, leeks, beans, garbanzos (often mixed with carrots), tomato and pepper sauces, eggs served in tomato sauce, chicken, lamb seasoned generously with garlic, *chorizos*, tongue, pig feet, *paella* (saffroned rice with chicken and/or seafood), potato *tortillas* (a thick potato and egg omelet sliced in wedges), and the popular olive oil, white vinegar, garlic, sugar, salt, and pepper salad dressing usually poured over plain, torn, iceberg lettuce. Fruit is the most common dessert, although *arroz con leche* (rice pudding), and *flan* (a baked custard with caramel sauce), and *tostadas* (a fried custard) are also popular. Fresh bread and wine, always red, are served at every dinner and supper. At Christmas, many women prepare fruit, particularly apples, in wine.

Another popular food for many Basque Americans is chestnuts. Martina Ibarra and her sister Alicia Farmer told me (interview, 22 June 1993) that one of their favorite winter suppers consists of warm roasted chestnuts accompanied by milk. Lucy

Echegary also mentioned the chestnut suppers. All of the Basque women I asked about preparing chestnuts suggested the same method for preparation. They first soak the chestnuts, nick them with a knife, and bake them in a moderate oven until the skin begins to peel away. I asked if they were really that easy to prepare, and they laughed and thought it was incredible that I had never prepared a chestnut. They said that the chestnut and milk supper was common during their childhoods in the old country and it is still a favorite meal, but chestnuts have become very expensive. Martina Ibarra mentioned that on her last few visits to the old country she observed fewer chestnut trees than there once were. "Everything is changed, even the chestnut trees," she said.

I asked many women if they had any difficulty finding specific ingredients for their ethnic cooking. The answers varied according to the region. Overall there does not seem to be a problem; however, for those in the more remote sections of Idaho, obtaining items like saffron, dried cod, or squid is nearly impossible without advance planning. Fortunately, the butchers are usually willing to special order items. With the influence of Chicana/Chicano residents in Idaho, the grocery markets are stocking more varieties of peppers and other typically Spanish ingredients. Now, Basque Americans in the Idaho desert, far from the Sea of Biscay, can prepare and enjoy menu items like squid in ink sauce and *chorizos* almost as often as they want them.

Basque American women combine ingredients from traditional Basque and mainstream American cooking styles. For instance, Dorothy Ansotegui (letter, 23 September 1993) said that her mother had never prepared a turkey for the American holiday of Thanksgiving until sometime in the late 1940s. Then her first turkey included dressing, but she improvised by adding ham, *chorizo*, and pimento to give it a Basque flavor. Julie Pagoaga of Shoshone, Idaho, mentioned to me that she has added saffron to various dishes to give them a more interesting flavor (conversation, 9 November 1993).

Cecelia Jouglard (interview, 20 March 1990) remarked as she served me the cod dinner in Rupert, "To understand the Basques, you must eat the food. Then you will understand our people." The food I have enjoyed has been intelligently prepared with thought and careful seasoning. Cecelia also said, "I think it, and then I cook it." Basque and Basque American cuisine celebrates the flavor of the food but does not overwhelm. It is, like the people, interesting and pleasurable.

Folk Dancing

Dancing is a vital part of Basque social life, both in the old country and in the United States. The dancing performed at the festivals in Idaho was largely the result of efforts by an elderly Basque American woman who lived in Boise, Idaho, for many years. I was introduced to the late Juanita Uberuaga Hormaechea at a traditional Basque restaurant in Boise (the Oñati). I had already observed her striking poise. Nicknamed Jay, she is referred to by some as the "mother of the Basque Dance," a title conferred on her by the Friends of the Idaho Historical Museum, 30 March 1993. Carrying herself with the erect bearing and energy of someone much younger, she enthusiastically reaffirmed an appointment I had made with her by telephone for the following day. I noted silently that this appointment in itself was remarkable because her husband had died just a week or so before. When I arrived at her home, I was again reminded of the inappropriateness of my timing by the presence of many plants and flowers from the funeral, but she received me graciously and stated that she was always glad to talk about the dance.

In that very brief interview (22 June 1993), she explained the philosophy behind her deep involvement in traditional Basque dancing in Boise. She said: "It brings the families together. It brings people together. The children dance, and the parents, grandparents, aunts, and uncles all come to watch. That

Dancers at *Jaialdi* 1990, Boise, Idaho.

is what is so important. It is something to help keep the families together. Something to have in common. Something to cele-brate." This great lady of the dance first offered the young Basque children of Boise and surrounding areas folk dancing lessons in 1947. The Boise *Oinkari* Basque Dancers—*Oinkari* meaning "one who does with his feet" or "dancers"—is an internationally known group of folk dancers established in 1960 by male and female performers who learned the traditional foot work of the complex dances from Jay. The group is often referred to as "the fast feet" by observers.

At *Jaialdi* '90 and '95, Basque American folk dancers wearing a variety of colorful costumes performed many intricate examples of these complex folk expressions. Dancers represented Basque clubs in Boise, San Francisco, Los Angeles, Chino, Reno, and other cities in the United States. There were also performers from the Basque Country who had traveled to Idaho to take part in the celebrations. They performed the popular *jota* and other complex traditional folk dances, including both the serious, majestic Spanish Basque dances and the gay, but complex dances of the French Basques.

The *godalet dantza*, or wine glass dance, was one of the most popular performed by both the *Oinkari* and other groups. I have seen it performed several times with little variation; the major performer, traditionally a male, wears a horse costume. When he is close to the glass, the costume prevents him from seeing either the full glass of wine or his feet. The full wine glass is in place to challenge his spatial judgement, skill, balance, and luck. He locates the glass as he carefully dances closer and closer to it. He gently determines his distance from the glass by using the sides of his feet. Stepping briskly to the rhythm of the Basque *txistu* (flute) and *atabal* (drum), he quickly and lightly poises the soles of both of his leather slippers upon either side of the full glass. He then leaps up and with one foot makes the sign of the cross over the glass as he hops clear. Then, dancing backward from the glass with quick, tiny steps, he sways from side to side, turns, and joins the other members of the troop. Remember that all of this is performed with his feet entirely invisible to him because of the broad horse costume. When the dance is done correctly, the glass of red wine stands at the end as it did before. Ancient tradition attaches a year-long omen of good or bad luck to whether or not the glass is spilled, though this folk belief was not recognized among the women I interviewed. It may be that the only ones who recognize the lucky benefit of performing this dance perfectly are the dancers themselves.

I also observed an excellent demonstration of skill among Basque American children competing to win a wine glass dance contest at Nevada's Elko Basque Festival, 4 July 1993. Divided by age, both children and teenagers competed. Girls and boys danced gracefully and confidently amid cheers of praise and awe from relatives and hundreds of other onlookers. Though some young contestants spilled the wine, a surprising number of glasses remained standing.

The University of Nevada, Reno's Basque dance group, the *Zenbat Gara Dantzari Teldea* (How Many Are We?), made their debut in Reno in 1989. The group's resourceful and energetic director is Lisa Corcostegui. Lisa wrote, "We take great pride in our authenticity and accuracy. Most other groups, including *Oinkari*, do modify and even rechoreograph. The fact that we do not sets us apart" (letter, 10 April 1994). The group researches and often takes patterns from garments preserved in Old World museums. In a recent article about the Basque dance, Nevada writer Joan Brick states:

> Many Basque dances performed today in the United States differ from their performance in the Basque Country. Adherence to traditional style is dictated by each group. *Zenbat Gara* strives for authenticity and accuracy, while acknowledging the fact that changes may be necessary depending on the size of the group.

Zenbat Gara Basque Folk Dance Ensemble, University of Nevada, Reno. Photographs by Julia Ratti (*top*) and Megan Kiley (*bottom*).

Basque dancers perform at ethnic events such as festivals, conventions, and picnics. They enhance cultural programs at the schools. Nursing home residents are entertained by their colorful forms as they twirl and stomp. Shopping mall patrons pause to watch the dancers exhibit their talents during various ethnic celebrations. Basque hotels host lively performances. (1992, 8)

Isabel Jausoro and her husband Jimmy have been involved with the Boise folk dance groups since the beginning of formal lessons in 1947. Jimmy has been an active musician for sixty-five years, first learning to play the accordion in his parents' boarding house in Nampa, Idaho. He has arranged all of the music for the *Oinkari* group, and he has performed with the group at the Montreal, Canada, Exposition in 1970 and at Expo '74 in Spokane, Washington. His work and tremendous contribution to American culture was recognized publicly when, nominated by folklorist Steve Siporin of Utah State University, he received the National Endowment for the Arts Heritage Award in 1985 in Washington, D.C.

Isabel said (interview, 22 June 1993), "Music is his first love, and I have always enjoyed supporting him in it." They both accompanied the *Oinkari* on a tour through the Basque Country in 1985. The Basque government made arrangements for the group of sixty-five Basque Americans, and the dancers performed in every Basque province in Spain and France. Isabel stated that a cherished highlight of the tour was a day spent south of Bilbao in Basauri, which was called a "Day of Dancing." Folk dancers from both sides of the Pyrenees frontier performed beautiful dances all day long. There were costumes and performances, Isabel said, "like none I had ever seen before." She then noted, "Some of Lisa's dances for the new Reno group are similar to some I saw there."

The dance is one of the key elements in the socialization of the young Basque American children. Miren Artiach told me (interview, 12 October 1991) that she and other Basque American mothers are helping to "expand ethnic understanding among the Basque children of Boise by teaching folk dancing lessons to 150 children one afternoon and evening a week." The children perform in a yearly recital in Boise that is open to the public and well attended by parents, relatives, and friends. To the Basques, both in this country and in the old country, the *jota* and other dances are an integral part of their collective consciousness and its expression.

Basque American Organizations

A number of formal Basque American organizations have been established to help with ethnic maintenance and with communications between the various Basque communities of the West. The North American Basque Organization (NABO), the Basque Cultural Centers, the Society for Basque Studies in America, and a Basque Museum in Boise, Idaho, are only a few among many efforts being made. Both men and women are continuing to create new meanings and interpretations of their dynamic and negotiated Basque American identity. Conscious of their contributions to American life in the West and of the mutually supportive relationship between the cultures of the old country and America in establishing future directions, individuals have worked creatively to prevent the culture from being entirely assimilated by mainstream America. Janet Inda, a tireless tradition-bearer, is the only woman to have held the office of president of NABO. One of the organization's founders, she has served in many capacities. Virginia Argoita has served in several offices, including secretary and treasurer in the Reno club and as a delegate to the national NABO conventions. From extended interviews with these women in Nevada, and with Basque Club participants in Boise and San Francisco, I have constructed a partial picture of past and current efforts of women who have contributed to the success of these, and other key cultural organizations, including the Roman Catholic Church.

The Church

In generations past, Basques in both the rural and urban regions of northern Spain and southern France practiced devout Roman Catholicism. Though the churches and cathedrals still stand with open doors and solemnly garbed priests, the masses on Sunday mornings are poorly attended. The attending congregation is made up mostly of the elderly. A professor at the Universidad Del Pais Vasco in San Sebastian (anonymous interview, 10 July 1990) confessed that he was a pure Basque and a Catholic, but for him, the church had no meaning except for christening, marrying, and burial. This attitude is partly a legacy from the Spanish Civil War. The Catholic church did not come to the rescue of the Basque Republicans when they resisted Franco's overthrow of the government; as a result, there are still dregs of resentment in the Basque people. Further, the active participation in church has steadily decreased as the society has become more comfortable and affluent under a democratic government. This contrasts with the attitudes of many Basque American women I interviewed throughout the western United States. The tradition of the church and participation in its many rituals remains one of the unifying ethnic markers of Basque American families.

Though the ideology of power some still attribute to Basque women is perceived by others to be a myth, the emotional and physical investment in the church, schools, and community which many of these women make in behalf of their husbands and children is powerful and influential. Often well educated and well informed and often displaying soft, well-modulated voices and immaculate grooming, these women traditionally set aside their own careers, often professional, to serve of their families and their communities. Earlier in this paper I mentioned asking Carmelo Urza about the supposed mystic power of Basque women. His comment about women ruling was meant jokingly, but there is a folk belief held by many of the people with whom I talked about the power, or perhaps loving control, that many women seem to have in their family domain. Most of these women take the church and their commitment to transferring the Catholic faith to the next generation seriously.

As was mentioned above, for centuries in the old country Basque women were allowed great responsibilities in the Catholic church. This was true of other cultures in Europe as well. Women parishioners were responsible for the spiritual well-being of the members of their households, both living and dead. It was the responsibility of the *serora* (female assistant to the priest) to receive bread and candles brought to the church by women as offerings in behalf of the souls of their dead ancestors. The role of the *serora* in today's Basque-Catholic churches in the old country has been devalued, and there are fewer and fewer people who keep the traditions, but the strong sense of responsibility assumed by the women concerning the church and their family members has not. Attending mass regularly to be instructed through the homily and to partake of the wine and wafer of communion are weekly rituals for most of these households.

Though many of the old religious customs may be dim memories for some and completely unknown to others, most of the Basque American women I interviewed respected Catholic tradition and have established conventions and activities, both conservative and dynamic, to help creatively communicate to their children a sense of what it means to be American, Basque, and Catholic. Conventional Catholic behavior included attending parochial schools and universities, attending mass weekly or even more often, noting the period of Lent spiritually, using Roman Catholic iconography in the home, and observing saints' and fast days with appropriate fasting and attendance at mass.

Festivities at the many three-day Basque American festivals held in California, Idaho, and Nevada between May and

September include a Sunday morning mass. Often held outdoors, the mass is conducted by a French Basque or Spanish Basque priest who celebrates it in both English and Basque. One of the important parts of the Basque mass is a ritual surrounding the offering. At that time, young children in Basque ethnic costumes reverently carry baskets of fruits, vegetables, breads, and other foodstuffs to the altar, and the priest receives them. It is a time of smiling exchanges between the children and the priest and a moment for the congregation to enjoy the beauty and innocence of the children and their offerings.

Education

Education for their young has always been important to the Basque American people. Most of the married couples from the old country who have established themselves here consider themselves Americans and have no plans to leave; therefore, they consider it very important for their children to receive an American education, including English. Victoria Barrutia, of Boise, Idaho, described (interview, 23 June 1993) her early education between 1915 and 1920 in Dry Creek, north of Boise. Her father and his five brothers had all come from Vizcaya, and they established a family sheep operation. Since they were all married and had children (most of them married women from the old country), they built a school house and imported a teacher from Boise. The many cousins attended the school together for several years, but eventually the families moved into Boise and the children entered schools there. The cousins have kept in touch with each other as they grew older, and today they maintain their contact with one another through a cousins' club that meets in Boise each year for a large family reunion.

Benedicta Cendagorta Elorza, of Reno, Nevada, explained (interview, 11 June 1993) how children who lived on widely scattered sheep ranches in Idaho and Nevada were educated. Because Benedicta's father was a sheepman he traveled often, and she used to accompany him as often as possible. They would travel across

Victoria Barrutia, Boise, Idaho.

territory between Idaho and Nevada. She observed firsthand how many isolated ranch families lived and educated their young. Usually a teacher would be hired and provided with a place to live. "The children from different areas came there, not too many, but that's where they had their classes...The teacher lived there, and the kids...would come there and go home in the evening." When the children got older, they were often sent into town to live with relatives and to attend high school. Some of the young women stayed on in town and attended business school.

Many of the second-generation Basque American women I interviewed, born between 1900 and 1935, were not able to attend school beyond seventh or eighth grade because of the isolation of the ranches. No regret was expressed about that; to the contrary, the women expressed pride in their long records of hard work and equally in the educations they have provided for their own children. Three women I interviewed in a group in Reno, Nevada, said that none of them had completed high school; each had one son, and the sons were all professionals. One son was a dentist and instructor in Oklahoma City, one was an elementary school teacher in Reno, and one was a veterinarian in Canada.

In Rupert, Idaho, the benefit dinner and dance mentioned above originally began many years ago as a parish fundraiser by the Basque ladies of St. Ann's Altar Society of the St. Nicholas Catholic Church. It has grown into a community event that also raises money for St. Nicholas School. Originally the dinner was held in the church hall, but due to its increased reputation, it had to be moved to a larger facility. Kathy Etcheverry has been chairman of the event for fourteen years and states that since moving the dinner to the Rupert Elks Hall, not only is the dinner served family style but also the organizers have added the auction-raffle and dance. In addition to the lucrative sheepherder's bread mentioned earlier, a Basque beret may be auctioned for eighty to a hundred dollars. A "phantom lamb" is often donated for the auction, and it is sometimes resold eight to ten times for a total of around $2,000.

Kathy wrote (letter, 17 February 1994), "I feel this is the largest *community* supported event; we serve at least 500 people in a two hour period." Kathy said that the number of Basque women participating in the cooking has greatly decreased, but the food is prepared as closely as it can be to genuine Basque style. Jean Etcheverry Chisholm, Kathy Etcheverry, and Alicia Dredge, all of whom have children who attended the school formerly, donate time to the various aspects of the festival. The net profit from this church/school fundraiser is divided equally between the altar society and St. Nicholas School.

The daughters and the granddaughters of the women I interviewed have pursued a broad spectrum of non-professional and professional training and education. Many of the daughters were sent to Catholic boarding schools in Salt Lake City and in Oregon during their high school years. That experience was often followed by higher education at private Catholic schools such as Notre Dame, Gonzaga, Seattle, Portland, and San Francisco universities. On the other hand, many second and third generation women I interviewed obtained educations in public schools and state universities. A significant number had studied, or at least spent time, in the Basque Country in either Spain or France. A few returned to the Basque Country after completing their undergraduate degrees in order to continue their study of Basque. Some support themselves by working as English teachers in the Basque school system.

Denise Inda was born in Reno, Nevada, in 1968. Her father, Michel, is from the French side of the Basque frontier, and her mother is Janet, whose father Pierre came from Basse Navarre. After completing an engineering degree, Denise taught conversational English in an *ikastola*, or Basque school, near Bilbao and studied advanced Basque in the evenings. She graduated from both the College of Idaho at Caldwell (now Albertson College) and the University of Nevada, Reno, with majors in engineering and art and minors in Spanish and Basque. After completing her core courses at Caldwell, Denise chose to study Spanish in the Basque Country. She received generous scholarships that covered every expense except for room and board. Denise decided, after arriving in northern Spain, to study Basque instead of Spanish. She subsequently immersed herself entirely in the country and its language. Arrangements were made for her to live with a Basque-speaking family, she audited her Spanish, and she participated in rigorous year-long Basque language study in San Sebastian. After the close of the spring semester, Denise studied at a *barnetegi*, a Basque language center about an hour and a half from San Sebastian. After studying

Denise Inda, Reno, Nevada.

there, she remained in the Basque Country for another month and a half and then returned to the United States to complete her engineering degree in Reno. After her graduation in December of 1992, she returned to the old country to study the language further at Lesaka. Denise described (interview, 14 June 1993) the students there as individuals who really want to learn the language, "people who feel that speaking Basque is important to being Basque." Though her educational focus is engineering, she knew she could not get an engineering position in Spain, so teaching was a means to the goal of mastering more of the Basque language.

At the annual Basque picnic in Elko, Nevada, 4 July 1993, I interviewed half-sisters who were born and raised in southeastern Idaho: Christine Landa and Elise Chisholm. Christine's father, a Basque immigrant who had acquired his own sheep business in Rupert, Idaho, was tragically killed in a highway accident when she was a small child. Her mother, after several years, married a young, American lawyer from a neighboring town in Idaho. In time, Elise was born to the second marriage. Christine, who is in her twenties, attended the University of San Francisco and is now a certified public account for Price-Waterhouse. When Christine first arrived in San Francisco, she attended the Basque Cultural Center and Club quite often, but as her circle of friends grew, she went to the center less frequently. Though she is interested in her Basque heritage and hopes to travel to the Basque Country for the second time in the not too distant future, at this point her professional commitments and interests related to her work are taking most of her time.

Elise graduated from high school in Minidoka County, Idaho, and now attends a Catholic women's college in the Midwest. She too is interested in her Basque heritage, but because she grew up so far from a Basque center, particularly where Basque dancing was taught, she had to focus in other directions. She hopes to learn more of her Basque heritage as she moves along in life.

Denise Inda, Elise Chisholm, and Christine Landa represent different educational disciplines, yet all are quite representative of the educational achievement among the second and third generation youth I interviewed.

Cultural Maintenance

Jerònima Echeverria informs us that when she and her family made regular Sunday visits to the Chino *Centro Basco* hotel, in California, her father participated in handball, her mother enjoyed visiting with friends, and the whole family enjoyed suppers on a long picnic table, yet, as she notes, "I cannot remember anyone ever pointing out that we went to the hotels to see our Basque friends, to experience our heritage, or to strengthen our ties to one another" (1988, 4). Echeverria suggests that the hotels at that time could have been considered an "invisible institution" so well "integrated into the Basque American culture that even the *Amerikanuak* (Basque Americans) were unlikely to distinguish them in their everyday life" (1988, 4).

In contrast, Denise Inda states that she has been conscious of her Basque American identity since she was a small child (interview, 14 June 1993). Denise was born in the late sixties, a period in the United States when public celebration of ethnicity was beginning to become a popular national activity. By that time, many Basque clubs had been established in the West, and conscious participation in the activities was an important part of her parents' focus in raising their only child. Denise particularly loved the Basque folk dances and remembers participating as a costumed dancer. Over a period of time, she met cousins and bonded strongly with them and with the many friends she met at various Basque American functions provided for the children. She remembered a Basque musician from the old country who was imported to teach in the children's music camps. In addition to songs and dances, he taught the folklore of the old country. The yearly summer music camps, two weeks long, are still held in the western states but in a different region each year in order to encourage all Basque American children to take part. When Denise was a child, her mother, Janet Carrica Inda, supported her interest fully by helping with the organizational responsibilities.

Janet Inda, whose French-Basque father came to America to herd sheep and eventually became an independent rancher, was deeply involved in establishing organizations to help maintain a sense of Basque identity and awareness. Janet (interview, 14 June 1993) expressed concerns she felt for Denise and other Basque American children while Denise was still a very young child. She said that she and others realized that "...if we do not do something [for the kids]...we will always be Basque because it's in our blood, but for the kids who are going to grow up now...if we don't show them their Basque heritage, there's not going to be anything left for them."

As ethnic revival movements began to arise during the sixties in the United States as well as in other Western nations such as Canada, the United Kingdom, Australia, and western Europe, ethnic rejuvenation became a popular phenomenon. What began to take place was what anthropologist Claude Levi-Strauss called bricolage. In *The Savage Mind*, he defined bricolage as an ongoing process in which new ideas are broken down, compared, and then synthesized with old ones (1966, 19). The scattered Basque American communities began to establish networks to provide more communication between themselves. These new links between the Basque clubs of Idaho, California, and Nevada were used to enhance their public image and to begin to more clearly define a Basque American identity. The Basque Americans joined with others in what is often called the roots phenomenon in order to reinforce and intensify ethnic identifications and allegiances. Folklorist Stephen Stern has stated,

> "Whereas most investigators concur the normal trend of acculturation favors the 'loss' of Old World folkloristic elements, they would agree that special

circumstances give rise to a revival of Old World folkloric expression" (1977, 17).

Cultural maintenance has taken many forms for Basque Americans. As discussed above, in the late 1940s Juanita Hormaechea began to give Basque folk-dancing lessons to children and youth in Boise, Idaho. During the 1950s, the Boise Basque Center was built, and in 1960, the *Oinkari* dancers of Boise were officially formed as a professional performing group. They performed at the Seattle World's Fair in 1962 and at the New York World's Fair in 1964. In a taped video interview made by Brad Larrondo, Jimmy Jausoro, the *Oinkari* accompanist, stated that after that, dance groups proliferated among the Basque American clubs. "Though," he said, "no two were alike. Every one was a little different" (Larrondo 1993, video).

As stated above, the first national Basque festival was held in 1959 in Sparks, Nevada, just outside of Reno. Douglass and Bilbao state that this "festival served as both a stimulus and model for future Basque festivals" (1975, 389). Presently, from May to September, ten festivals are held by different clubs in various cities in California, Nevada, and Idaho. The North American Basque Organization also sponsors *pelota* (handball) camps, directed by professional *pelota* coaches from the old country, *mus* (similar to poker) championship competitions, and an informative newsletter called *Hizketa*, which means "chat," or "talk," or "conversation." Besides news of activities and competitions, *Hizketa* includes articles about the history and literature of the Basques both in the old country and in the United States.

Janet Inda, who served two terms as president of the North American Basque Organization, a key element in Basque American identity formation and maintenance, stated (interview, 14 June 1993) that NABO was organized among other reasons: "In order to establish acquaintances among Basques from here, there, and everywhere." Suggesting that she got involved "through the back door," Inda explained some of her part in the founding of NABO. At the time NABO was begun, the Basque Studies Program at the University of Nevada, Reno, was in its infancy. In late 1971, while working in the special collections section of the University of Nevada, Reno, library, she received a telephone call from Al Erquiaga in Boise, Idaho, who had been given her name. "Erquiaga," Inda said, "was working in a job where he realized he could get a grant." He expressed concern that Basque Americans did not generally know of the Basque Studies Program and other efforts being made to preserve the Basque ethnic heritage, except those operating in their own locale. He wanted to learn if there was interest among Basque Americans in forming some sort of an organization to establish a genuine network of communities.

In a little time, some money for phone calls and stamps was made available, and Erquiaga, Miren Artiach (also from Boise), and Janet Inda began making phone calls. Janet said that they would use phone books from various cities and look for Basque names. After finding them, they would call the people and explain that they were young, American-born Basques trying to form a network between the various Basque groups and clubs. She stated: "We found out, over the ensuing six or eight months, that yes, there was an interest, especially in the areas where there were ... young Basques who had young children." Nearly all of the established clubs were for both men and women, although Janet knew of a Basque organization in Ontario, Oregon, which was established some years ago and is made up only of women.

Recognizing the need for funding, the Reno Basque club met at the Sante Fe restaurant in downtown Reno, and the membership donated money for postcards and stamps in order to invite representatives from various clubs to meet and form a structure for an umbrella organization. In Reno, in March 1963, after many phone calls and meetings with various Basque clubs, the North American Basque Organization, Inc., was founded. A September 1981 article written by Darlene Ammons and Janet

Inda for *The Basque Studies Program Newsletter* stated clearly the purposes of the organization:

> The group met in Reno again in June and resolved that NABO should function as a service organization to member clubs without infringing on the autonomy of each. NABO's prime purpose was to be the preservation, protection, and promotion of the historical, cultural, and social interests of Basques in the United States. The new organization was to sponsor activities and events beyond the scope of the individual clubs. It was also to promote exchanges between Basque Americans and the Basque Country. (1981, 4)

After the organization was formed, a picnic was held in Reno, and the San Francisco *Klika*, a club with a band and dancers, was invited to come and be a part of the festivities. People invited acquaintances and "little by little, it just kind of mushroomed out."

Another key person in the current maintenance of Basque American ethnicity is Lisa Tipton Corcostegui, formerly of Ontario, Oregon, and now living in Reno with her husband Enrike. Beside directing the Basque folk-dance ensemble in Reno, Lisa provides Basque dancing lessons for young members of the Reno Basque American community. Lisa, whose mother is Basque and whose father is not, met and married Enrike in the old country during her studies there. She and her husband both treasure their Basque heritage; each year they study one or two different regions of his homeland so as to represent them in festival dance performances. Lisa said (interview, 15 June 1993) that she started Basque dancing when she was about five. Lessons were held weekly in the basement of the local Catholic church, and she loved them. Instructors were usually teenagers who danced with the *Oinkari* in Boise. Lisa said that her group looked up to those dancers like they were gods. Though she turned to classical ballet, she remained involved by teaching Basque dancing to very young children. It was hard to stay involved with her own Basque dancing through her teen years because the only place for older youths to take lessons was Boise, and it was difficult to get there. Further, Lisa saw herself as an outsider not only because she was from Ontario but also because she did not have a Basque surname.

During her master's graduate studies in Spanish literature and language, Lisa researched particularly the history and adaptations of Basque Old World folk dances in the Laburdi region of southern France. Her research helps the Reno dance group costume and perform the less well-known folk dances with as much accuracy as possible, while realizing that the dances are dynamic and there are steps and arrangements that are probably gone forever. Lisa's work is already becoming known throughout the Basque American community. The dances are considered to be key elements in preserving the culture because dance is an enjoyable way to involve both children and youths. Many individuals, both in Reno and in Boise, spoke to me of Lisa's creative contribution. Now preparing for a Ph.D. in Basque studies, Lisa hopes to keep the lore of the Basque dance as a focus for her life work.

The Basque Museum and Cultural Center

The Basque Museum and Cultural Center was dedicated at the *Jaialdi* 1987 Festival in Boise, Idaho. The museum, housed in a small brick building which served at one time as a Basque boarding house, is located on Grove Street. It is situated between the large Basque Center, where meeting and social events are held, and the museum's annex which houses extensive holdings of Basque historical materials. Adelia Garro Simplot, a Basque American woman keenly interested in Basque community education, purchased and donated the little boarding house. She is a past president of the Basque Museum and is presently an honorary chairperson. In the *Jaialdi '90 Program Book*, she was quoted as saying, "the enthusiastic support of our volunteers and other community members has given us a special type of museum that

The Cyrus Jacobs-Uberuaga House, part of the Basque Museum and Cultural Center, Boise, Idaho.

cannot be found anyplace else. It is a lasting legacy of our Basque forbearers [sic]" (Arrizabala and Barinaga 1990, 31).

The little brick boarding house, now the Basque Museum and focal point of Grove Street, is furnished with many pieces of furniture and artifacts from the boarding house period of the structure. It was originally the Cyrus Jacobs-Uberuaga house and is Boise's oldest surviving building. It was built in 1864 by Jacobs, an early Boise merchant and one of Boise's first mayors. When the Uberuaga family owned the building, it served as a boarding house and social center for hundreds of Basque sheepherders.

The Cultural Center, located next to the brick museum, houses thousands of books donated to Boise Basques from the Basque government, the University of Idaho, and other groups; an audio-video library that includes music and historical films from the old country; musical and photographic collections; and an archive of materials on Basque dance. Basque language classes

National Monument to the Basque Sheepherder, Reno, Nevada.

have been held there and have been very well received by the Boise Basque community. Anyone interested in the history and culture of the Basque people is welcome to use the facility. The Basque Museum and Cultural Center are run by volunteers from the community, mostly Basque American girls and women, and the museum also has an informative newsletter that often includes articles about Basque history.

Another important organization that lends academic credence and honors individuals who contribute to the Basque culture in America is the Society of Basque Studies in America. This organization "seeks to gather and disseminate up-to-date knowledge regarding Basques worldwide so that others may learn of their distinctive heritage, ancient language, customs, and traditions" (Echeverria 1994, ii). The society was instrumental in sponsoring the National Monument to the Basque Sheepherd in Reno, Nevada, dedicated in 1989.

Txistu

Tanbolin

Afterword

I interviewed Bernard Landa, son of Jean Etcheverry Landa Chisholm, a few years ago when he was a senior engineering student at Notre Dame University. He is a full-blooded Basque, a third generation American, and the son of a French Basque sheepherder who died when Bernard was very young. Bernard told me that he really has no comprehension of what being a Basque means. He is an American, which is his only self-identity, though he does love his mother's and his amona's (grandmother's) ethnic cooking. "But Mom mixed it up with a lot of other types of cooking too. I am not at all sure what is Basque and what is not. It is all good."

Folklore that survives is kept because it serves useful purposes. Bernard's comments about his mother having "mixed it up" and "It is all good," are representative of an American generation that has lost a sense of its ethnic roots because of the mixing and sharing of cultures in our country. Finding common ground and sharing the varied contributions of our mixed-blood heritage is what we need to do in America; the mixing is good.

At the same time, however, many ethnic groups would like to keep alive the essence of their heritage in the midst of the mixing, and most members of the Basque American community think that it is worthwhile to continue their cultural traditions within an American context. Bernard and his sister Christine visited the Basque Country as young children and are planning to make another trip soon as young adults in an effort to inform themselves about their heritage. They will visit Bilbao in Vizcaya and see the new Guggenheim *Bilbao Museoa*. There Bernard and Christine will witness a blending of the American architect Frank Gehry's abstraction, a startling form, against the backdrop of a decaying but forward-thinking, changing industrial city. There, as in the United States, Basque and American expression are mixed. This brother and sister hope to transfer a sense of both past and present Basqueness to their future children. As Bernard said later, "I have a great heritage that I really don't know enough about. I want that" (interview, 20 November 1993).

The focus of this study has been the substantial contribution Basque American women of the western United States have made to the reinvention and maintenance of their dynamic cultural heritage. Their stories and perspectives have created an ongoing ethnic awareness that many of them cherish. Some, however, are struggling with unexpected changes in the interpretation of what it means to be a Basque American. The ancient Basque language either is being forgotten or is never learned in the first place by many second and third generation Basques in the United States. Few are able to continue sheepherding traditions or maintain the ranches they once had. Basque restaurants and hotels are few and far between, and even the few survivors are threatened with commercialization and trivialization of their former authentic purposes as gathering places. Young people like Bernard and Christine are entering American professional life and scattering throughout the nation, taking with them the youngest potential tradition-bearers, the grandchildren. But a

Basque quality of spirit and a ferocious desire by many to hold on to as much of the old as possible survives.

The collected narratives and stories presented here are a selection of the women's shared attempts to maintain and con-temporize a beloved ancient culture in a fast-paced, rapidly homogenizing American world. In fields such as folklore, history, sociology, and anthropology, the gathering of personal narratives has become a frequently used tool in the last half of the twenti-eth century for providing insight into individuals and cultures. Personal narratives differ markedly from statistical studies and surveys and from text- and document-centered research, because they lead us directly into the lives of real people with hopes, dreams, imaginations, specific agendas and complex strategies. The personal narratives of Basque American women share the complexities of their existence and invite their audience to join them in the joy and celebration of their culture. These lively voices recognize a part of their identity that they do not want their posterity to lose, and they are willing to work to maintain the integrity of their ideas: blending Old World essence success-fully with the new.

Though this text has focused on Basque American women, the implications for the study reach beyond the bound-aries of the Basque American culture. For several years, America has been trying to change her national metaphor. Since the beginning of the twentieth century, the prevailing imagery for cultural identity in our nation has been the melting pot. But that metaphor has failed and will continue to fail. Americans are not going to melt together into one cultural pudding. There has been and will continue to be some cultural blending, but there is no indication that the Christians, Jews, Hindus, Moslems, Buddhists and other religious groups of the nation are going to melt into one national religion. There is no indication that Native Americans, African Americans, Asian Americans, Euro-Americans, Basque Americans, and others are going to liquidize their genotypes, phe-notypes, and inherited symbols and practices together and become one type with a collective culture. It simply is not going to happen. The Basque American people, men and women, provide an example of how to become full-fledged, participating Americans and yet maintain a proud connection to their country of origin. What is an appropriate new metaphor for America? Possibly a cultural anthology? America is a collection, both thematic and at random, of people with stories and personal narratives. The popular salad bowl metaphor doesn't seem to work (at least for me) because the first question that comes to mind is what kind of dressing would be appropriate. That seems to imply a common denominator to make the flavor all the same. The stew metaphor doesn't work either. With that one, we too often reach for the salt and pepper to change the flavor without even sampling the taste. The most important question: "How do we maintain our uniqueness and still find common ground?" calls on our accountability and commitment to being democratic Americans.

The United States census of 1990 numbers the Basques of America as a separate ethnic group, and it enumerates a population of over 50,000. Basques, at an early date, gained a reputation throughout the western states as hard-working, honest Americans, and they have enlarged that reputation by contributing positively to many fields in both the private and public sectors. Pete Cenarrusa, a Basque who has been secretary of state in Idaho for many years, has worked diligently to help Basque Americans inform the greater American public about who and what they are. Basque restaurants, festivals, and other ethnic activities welcome non-Basques. In the last several years, realizing that other ethnic groups feel as strongly about preserving their unique identities as the Basques and realizing the advantages in combining ethnic festivals, Basque Americans have been involved in mixed cultural celebrations. In Brad Larrondo's video about the Basques of Boise, Dan Ansotegui, grandson of the Basque woman of Hailey, Idaho, who proudly served Colonel Sanders Basque fried chicken and owner of the Bar Gernika on Grove Street, in Boise, Idaho, states:

I don't think any one culture can stand on its own, especially in this country. We need to act together and enrich other cultures as well as enriching our own. We see a lot more of these things with the Mexican Americans that have their festival, and they include other cultures within that. The Greek festival is getting larger and larger every year, and the Basque festival is becoming revitalized. I think those things are important to us, but in order for them to continue to grow, we need to include everybody in those. We can't just be the Basques anymore.

Two community festivals which feature mixed ethnic heritages are held annually in Walla Walla, Washington, and in Boise, Idaho. For the last several years, the Italian festival planners in Washington have wanted demonstration dancers, and no Italian dancers have been available. Therefore, they imported the *Oinkari* Basque folk-dance group from Boise. Their group's regular accompanist, Jimmy Jausoro, also provided lively music with his accordion. In Boise, the Green River Festival features many cultures of the city. People share the foods, sounds, and colors of several traditions.

Elliott Oring, in his text *Folk Groups and Folklore Genres*, suggests that "members of an ethnic group ... share and identify with a historically derived cultural tradition or style" and that ethnic identity is "the intellectual and emotional sense that an individual has of his relationship to the behaviors, ideas, and values of an ethnic group" (1986, 24). Many Basque American women, young and old, do not mind inventing a new sense of ethnicity as long as it has a Basque flavor, as long as they can still identify with historical cultural tradition and still retain a sense of their relationship to their group. It is not unlike turkey dressing flavored with *chorizos* and pimento or lasagna enlivened with saffron. The continuing presence of an unmistakable Basqueness seems to be enough for many families. Others resist weakening and dilution of their Basque identity. However strong their cultural tenacity, most of the women preserve a sense of ethnic integrity by repeatedly blending the old with the new, and maintaining discerning and powerful beliefs in education and family. They share values with much of the general society around them but enjoy the challenge of maintaining their distinctly Basque characteristics and symbols.

The collective memories of older Basque Americans influence the younger generation, but it is impossible to project what the long-term results will be. I have visited with many young men and women, who ranged in age from ten or twelve to about thirty, at various Basque American festivals and other activities associated with this study. Though many of them had not yet visited the old country, they spoke of themselves as Basques and accepted proudly their heritage from the Old World as Basque Americans. Frank Dredge, the now teenaged son of Alicia Dredge and her American husband, Cal, and grandson of French Basque sheepherder Frank Jouglard, said that he was very proud to be a Basque. At a Basque mass in Boise in 1990, where the *Oinkari* dancers performed in the sanctuary, he chastised me, when he was still a young boy, to put more money in the offering plate. "After all," Frankie said, "it is a Basque mass; it is worth more than five dollars." Frank continues to live part of the year at his parents' ranch in Caribou County, Idaho, and part of the time in town in his grandmother's home in Rupert. He has no exposure to the Basque Club in Boise nor is he a part of any dance group. He has never attended the music camp. Neither does he particularly like Basque food. And yet, by being raised by his storytelling grandmother, Cecelia Jouglard, and his well-educated mother, Alicia, he has drawn an identity for himself from the memories of their experiences. Through books and language, by absorbing the memories spoken of by his mother and grandmother, the boy has become a thorough Basque American. His intensity may wane as he grows older; that remains to be seen. For the present, he is a proud Basque American male.

Young people like Frank Dredge sense something within them which they name Basque, and they feel good about that identity. But what will it mean to him later?

For some years, I have had a professional association with a young Basque American author in the Intermountain West. He has helped me immeasurably with this study and others because he believes in the preservation of the culture. The last time he wrote to me was to ask my support for a project he was conducting. I gave it and then called later to see how it all turned out. When he answered the phone, he did not sound like the same man. I asked if I could help, and he said, "Probably not. Thanks anyway. I seem to be going through some kind of identity thing. It has something to do with family, and being Basque, and not being sure that is where I am all the time and ..." (Anonymous).

The United States is going through its own cultural identity crisis. With changing demographics and a growing economy, the country has reached a point where new immigrants from Asia, Africa, and Latin America are all struggling to find their place. They ask the same questions. How does a group hold onto its uniqueness but at the same time gain a respectable toehold in the consumer economy of North America? Certainly much depends on intergenerational maintenance of tradition. Janet Inda states: "The future of our Basque American culture is in the hands of the youth. If we don't teach them the value of their heritage, we will lose all we have worked for to maintain it. I trust them to guard it" (interview, 14 June 1993). Guarding and maintaining it has often required reinventing it. Basque Americans are a generally successful example of how an ethnic group can shape American identity, but the issue arises anew with each generation.

One young Basque American musician, Jean Louis Curutchet, told me at the Winnemucca Basque Festival that, like many other Basques, his father had been a successful landscape gardener in San Francisco for several decades. A new influx of immigrants has seriously threatened his and other established landscaping businesses. Many of the immigrants, seeking a toe-hold, habitually underbid on jobs, and the customers usually go with the lowest bid. Their work, Jean Louis says, is not the same quality as his father and other experienced landscapers perform. The consequence is, nevertheless, that the business is lost. The family is discussing a probable relocation at some time because Jean Louis's economic future is dependent on the business surviving. His hope is that the family will be able to relocate in a predominantly Basque area in Idaho or Nevada (interview, 13 June 1993). Such change, though, can weaken the ethnic bonds of younger family members.

Change is often a source for conflict and difficult adjustment no matter how logical or natural it may be. Janet Inda mentioned (telephone interview, 6 December 1993) unfortunate, but perhaps inevitable conflict between some of the young adults and the older people in a few of the Basque clubs in the West. It has taken many years to build the Basque Cultural Centers in Boise and in San Francisco. Of course, the land and buildings were expensive and were primarily purchased and built with donations from hard-working first-generation immigrants. Many of the younger members of the Basque clubs would like to rent the buildings out for various functions in order to make the maximum amount of money from each structure. They see no point in having the buildings stand idle part of the time. Many of the older members are adamant about not renting the buildings to strangers. It was primarily their sacrifices that built the clubs initially, and they do not want them used for anything but Basque functions.

Some of the battles over these issues have become extraordinarily heated. Change and youthful enthusiasm threatens to disrupt older, traditional folkways that are now only a remnant of what they were like in the days when there were many boarding houses and hotels. In those days, the aroma of garlic and onion filled the air, *pelota* courts buzzed with activity, and the sounds of the language and the music provided a haven. Those were connections, and now they are common memories. The young remember only vaguely or not at all. "Remembrances are mutually supportive of each other and common to all," Maurice Halbwachs states (1950, 48), and in this instance, older Basques remember the Great Depression, the hard times, the old hotels, foods, bare survival, and the shared language. Younger Basque Americans remember the music camps with their music, stories, dances, laughter, snippets of language, and the freedom and excitement of being children together.

Shared memories among the younger Basque Americans have led to deep friendships and even occasional marriages. Theirs is a different perception of what it means to be Basque American. The first generation of campers is now in their twenties. From Southern California to northern Oregon and Idaho, these young adults know and respect one another; they were children together in the camps. Early bonds were forged, and they are now reinforced through the many yearly festivals, through paths that cross during their university studies both in the United States and in the Basque Country, and through newsletters and other publications. Information is widely disseminated through the newsletters of NABO, the Basque Studies Program at the University of Nevada, Reno, and local club letters.

Janet Inda described (interview, 6 December 1993) a marriage between a young couple who were both graduates of music camps. John Ysura, now a professor in California, and Jenny Petresans, a school teacher, met at a music camp in Boise. John was a member of the Boise *Oinkari* dancers, and Jenny grew up dancing with the Basque club in Chino, California. After they married, their intense interest in the dancing led them to spend a year in Europe conducting research concerning folk dance, costuming, and music. Their research was funded, in part, by NABO. Their intention is to give back to the Basque American culture even more than they were given as children in the music camps and later in the dance groups.

Monique Laxalt Urza (interview, 15 June 1993) discussed what it means to unravel the threads of one cultural identity and weave them into another. "It is more difficult and complex than most people realize," Monique told me as we visited in the garden behind her Reno home. "I am an American, and so are my children. Having been raised here, they have a natural sense of American identity." Monique explained her concern for the dangers of creating a mythical heritage for Basque Americans which is difficult to reconcile with the reality of modern-day American life. She takes her children to Basque-sponsored functions, but has tried to strike a balance between Basque and American identity. She said that living in the old country for extended periods while her father was researching and writing some of his books led her to a clearer understanding of her grandparents and their points of view. Observing what life might have been for them, she understood the reasons they may have wanted to leave their homeland. "It is not just a fairyland, but rather, it is a very real society with very complex problems, just as is any society. It is important that children have a firsthand, real sense of the country of their heritage."

Immigration is a long process, Monique said, and it affects each generation in a different way. People, their character building, and their negotiations with reality are works in progress. Monique indicated that in the old country, relatives are simple people to whom one is always related. People do not particularly work at relationships among family members as many do in America. "There are just automatic ties, and they are permanent; no one worries about them." In her family, Monique concluded, the philosophy is to look forward as well as backward. She feels that looking forward to and supporting the choices her children make is as important as building a sense of Basque heritage with them.

Most of the women interviewed realize that many cultural traditions have already been lost in the acculturation process; the language, a key element of the Basque people, obviously has little use in American society. It is threatened with loss in the next few generations of Basque Americans because of its difficulty and because most of the youth have only a second-hand knowledge of the Old World culture. Third-generation youth have American-born, English-speaking parents. The challenge of keeping in the minds of the young a culture and a language they have never experienced would inevitably fail entirely without a continued adaptable and inventive attitude. Even though the parents and leaders know that the language will rarely, if ever, be mastered by fourth- and fifth-generation children in America, the efforts to establish the importance and uniqueness of the language have not stopped. Linked to a proud concept of Basque heritage, some women have expressed a fear that if it is entirely lost, the main key to the culture will be lost.

Various ways to preserve the language in the United States have been explored, and creative approaches are constantly being undertaken. One important method is the establishment of Basque American choirs in several of the Basque cultural centers or clubs. In mastering the songs of the Basque Country, the choir members learn many Basque words and rhythms. In the many Idaho, Nevada, and California homes where I interviewed first and second generation women, the language is spoken and openly cherished. These women do not want their posterity to lose touch with something they revere so much. They entertain their grandchildren with stories and words from the Basque homeland. Miren Artiach, of Boise, Idaho, spoke about the efforts she and her husband are making to teach their children to speak the Basque language in their home. She spoke of many other young couples who live in the Boise region who are doing the same thing. She said that it is a difficult and challenging task, but one the family is working on together with great satisfaction. Her children have ethnic pride, a sense of humor, and are cooperative with efforts to teach them (14 June 1990).

Some of the other parents are not having as positive an experience as Artiach. She told of one family that has found, because of outside influences and interference, more frustration than satisfaction with their effort to teach the language in the home. That family's children are not as reachable or as teachable since they became teenagers. However, the parents have not given up, and they know that even if the teenagers do not study further with their nuclear family, a foundation in the language has been established.

Unlike many other Basque Americans, Janet Inda does not see language as necessarily the most important part of the culture. She recognizes that is an unpopular point of view among many Basque Americans, young and old, but after all, this is America. Janet said, "This is where the young people are, this is where they are staying and if they are going to keep the heritage, they will slowly change the ideology" (interview, 14 June 1993). What was important to the older Basques is not necessarily most important to the younger ones.

We have entered a period in the United States when marked changes in the overall demographics of the country have become an issue of discussion, and even a threat, to many. The American Council on Education and the Education Commission of the States published, in 1988, a report called *One-Third of a Nation*. The report states that by the year 2000, one-third of the population of the United States will consist of non-white Americans (4). I have stated that the Basque American women are ethnic by choice. Many cultures in the United States do not have that choice, and the continuing problem is that many white Americans do not seem to grasp the concept that an immigrant Asian, East Indian, Mexican, or African can be just as American as they.

The Basques, as a minority group in America with typically European coloration, have not been forced to negotiate the race issue. They have easily blended into the mainstream culture, giving them decided advantages over many other ethnic groups in the United States. This is not to say that survival was not difficult but that there were additional advantages. To begin with, many Basques who came to the United States were sponsored by relatives or close friends, and they came here secure in knowing they had jobs. Secondly, their work ethic and use of time was very like the typical Puritan work ethic, and they quickly won the respect of like-minded Anglos. They are frugal, extraordinarily clean, healthy, and wholesome looking, mainly, I think, due to their enjoyment both of the outdoors and hard work. The young professionals I met, most of whom spend week days in offices, schools, or universities, are typical of a generation of health-conscious Americans and take great care of their bodies. Their physical activities range from strenuous biking to handball to fast-footed dancing and competitive swimming.

Like other ethnic groups in the United States, Basque Americans are seeking ways to keep their unique identity alive within the broader American society, but for them, there exists an aura of fun in the process that some other ethnic groups cannot yet embrace. Basque Americans appear to have more resources to invest in preserving their heritage in America because they entered the society easily, most had jobs from the beginning, and they have also received some funding for projects from the Basque autonomous government. There is much the Basques do not have in common with other strong American ethnic pluralities, but because they are yet very much in favor of their own ethnic survival and the survival of other groups, they may overcome those differences by combining the celebrations of ethnicity with those of other groups as in the deliberate cross-cultural mixing Dan Ansotegui suggested. However, in an uncomfortable interaction with assimilation realities, Basque Americans are also realizing that through intermarriage, family separations, and relocations, the heart of their culture in the West is weakening. Through hard work and education, Basques have become mainstream Americans and are just now grasping what that really means to the culture they love to celebrate.

The older members of the society are threatened and uncomfortable. Janet Inda noted that older members are quitting leadership positions in one of the cultural clubs because they claim they "cannot handle how the young think," and younger members have been quoted as saying they cannot handle "stodgy, older, single-minded attitudes" (interview, 14 June 1993). Many of the older Basque Americans seem to be attempting to hold on to a cultural essence that was really left behind nearly a century ago. The customs they and their parents brought with them from the old country, as Monique Urza pointed out, simply do not survive in the minds of the younger generation. The youth who study in the old country see the landscape and its people, both urban and rural, with American judgments and through an American lens. Industrialization in northern Spain has changed the face of Basque culture so radically that even in hamlets and villages tucked among hidden hills and valleys of the Pyrenees, television aerials, power lines, and other evidences of modern civilization abound. Unfortunately, brackish water runs in some of what were, just a few short decades ago, clear mountain streams. The consensus language, *Batua*, has been established but is sometimes called the "language of the Yuppies" (del Valle's lectures 1990).

The nineties is a time of international unrest and ethnic cleansing. There is perhaps as much nationalistic introspection occurring now as at any other time in the history of the world. A world economy is struggling to establish itself, and within that global neighborhood, each nation is trying to decide what it wants its part to be. Basque Americans, men and women, are not alone in their painful self-examination of what they are and where they are going as a culture.

Informed "travelers" and "intimate outsiders," as William Douglass calls himself, are cautiously optimistic about the future of Basque American culture in the United States. Douglass, warning gently of the dangers of speculation about someone else's future, does permit himself to make some projections. Briefly summarizing much of what has been accomplished to celebrate Basque American ethnic identity over the last forty years, Douglass pointed out (address 9 October 1993) that there are now "more vehicles for expression of Basque American identity than any time in the nearly one hundred and fifty years since Basques

first began to enter the American West" (17). Many of these vehicles are strong and appear to be ongoing. However, rather than
basing a rosy forecast on these organizations and events, Douglass
suggests that perhaps what might be taking place is an "Indian
summer of Basque American culture, a brief if glorious period
before its demise, at least as presently constituted" (17). Based on
changing demographics, intermarriage between Basques and non-
Basques, diminishing mastery of the language in the United
States, and "the externalization and commercialization of the ethnic identity," the Basque culture in the West risks becoming trivi-
alized. Douglass posits that unless the culture looks forward from
its past inspiration of "a European peasant heritage and American
sheepherding legacy," it "runs the risk of becoming more show
than substance" (23). He noted that recent and increasing
exchanges of people and cultural ideas between the Basque
Country and America have replaced the economic exchanges of
the last ethnic-reinforcing sojourner herders in the 1960s and
1970s. American and Basque students now seek instruction in
each other's universities, Basque trade delegations and government officials have visited the United States, performing artists
from the old country have participated in western American festivals, and Basque American performers have danced in the
provinces of Basque Spain and France. Out of this recent two-
directional cultural flow, Douglass cautiously projects, "the Basque
American identity of the twenty-first century is likely to emerge if
it is to emerge at all" (25).

The unique and mysterious origins of the Basques remain
an important part of the Basque American cultural self-identity.
Long ago when Sabino Arana wrote the first nationalist formula-
tions, he ascribed race as the core element of Basque uniqueness.
Studies continue, as noted in an earlier chapter, to confirm or
disavow that biological claim. Whether it is true or not, the facts
remain that for whatever reason, because of isolation or because
of failure to be conquered by an outside aggressor, most of the
Basque Americans and Basques whom I interviewed believe that

they have unique genetic characteristics in addition to the heritage of a mysterious language.

The women I interviewed are not optimistic about the future of their ethnic culture in America. They are informed about the cultural and educational exchanges between the Basque Country and the United States, Canada, and Mexico. Tradition-bearers ranging in age from their middle forties to their early nineties, these women foresee the future through their grandchildren. These youngsters, the grandmothers know, have little, if any, knowledge of what it is to be a part of the collective Basque American experience. On 11 June 1993, Cassie Duarte—a resident of Reno and child of a widowed, almost destitute mother who was left in the 1930s with seven young children in a desolate region of Nevada with no money and little hope—spoke for all of the older women I interviewed when she said: "Those early days are gone. We worked hard, and we lived on nothing, but we had each other. Even so, it was a good life. It is changed now. My son is a dentist and teacher in Oklahoma City, and he is married to a non-Basque girl. He and his family have an American life, and that's okay. That is what I worked for."

Basque Americans are fortunate because they know, clearly, where their roots are. They can go back to the old country and touch their father's chairs; they can hear, see, and even taste the world of their heritage. They are fortunate too, because their mothers have spread the table of America's abundance before them and have taught them to practice values and mores that help them produce and enjoy that abundance. Whether the language survives or not in the United States may be irrelevant. There is a new generation of tradition-bearers, young women (and young men) with collective memories of the music camps, study in the old country, dancing at the festivals, and maintaining life-long Basque American friendships. They are the caretakers, the cultural architects, of the next generation of Basque Americans. I believe the legacy of this unique, syncretic culture will be safely shaped and transmitted and will continue well into the future.

Notes

1. In a few villages of the Basque provinces of Navarra and Guipúzcoa, there are special serenades sung to a bridal pair on their wedding-night, or more usually on the day when their banns of marriage are published in church. Extolling the virtues of the bride and bridegroom, this stanza acknowledges the proclaimed equality between the sexes. For a more complete discussion of folk-songs, see Rodney Gallop, *A Book of the Basques* (Reno: University of Nevada Press, 1930, 1979), pp. 109–159.

2. Stephen A. Tyler reminds his readers that the "consumed fragments" of the information we as field workers attempt to collect can only be an evoking of "the other as us" (128). He suggests that the ethnographer shares with the subjects "means of experience" (138). In writing about the subjects, Tyler calls ethnography a "meditative vehicle … a start of a different kind of journey" (140). His article, "Post-Modern Ethnography: From Document of the Occult to Occult Document," is in *Writing Culture: The Poetics and Politics of Ethnography*, James Clifford and George E. Marcus, eds. (Berkeley: University of California Press, 1986), 128, 138, 140.

3. Teresa del Valle, 1990, "Women's Power in Basque Culture, Practice, and Ideology." In this paper, del Valle quotes her translation of A. Ortiz Oses, E. Borneman, and F. K. Mayr *Antropologia vasca simbolos, mitos y arquetipos*. n.d. Teresa del Valle referred to Ortiz and his hypothesis of the early Basque matriarchy in several of her lectures in July and August, 1990. In her essay, del Valle, a self-avowed radical feminist, posits that Ortiz Oses's argument of an early Basque matriarchy "is weak, highly speculative and difficult to maintain from an anthropological viewpoint." However, she stated, "the interest shown in Basque society and the popular acceptance of those theories is what is most interesting." (28)

4. Sandra Ott, *The Circle of the Mountains: A Basque Sheepherding Community* (Reno: University of Nevada Press, 1981, 1993). 103. Ott states: "Until 1962, when the present priest abolished the practice, the blessed bread ritual was performed every Sunday and consisted of two parts. The first part took place in the church or chapel, between which the High Mass alternated weekly. The second was performed in the houses of the bread-giving *etxekandere* (woman of the house) and her first 'first neighbor'."

5. The words of the prayer are spelled as Juan Garetea dictated them in his telephone interview with the author. The spelling has been criticized by Basque language scholars; however, it will remain as given.

6. Fred Davis, *Yearning For Yesterday: A Sociology of Nostalgia* (New York: Free Press, 1979), 33. Fred Davis states that "In the clash of continuities and discontinuities with which life confronts us, nostalgia clearly attends more to the pleas for continuity, to the comforts of sameness and the consolations of piety." Piety, that is, in the sense employed by Kenneth Burke: ". . . remaining loyal to the sources of one's being"; Kenneth Burke, *Permanence and Change*. Los Altos, Calif.: Hermes, 1954), 71–74.

Works Cited

Ammons, Darlene and Janet Inda. 1981. "Forging a Link: The North American Basque Organization, Inc." *The Basque Studies Program Newsletter* (September): 4–6.

Anonymous. 1989. Interview by author. Rupert, Idaho. 16 March.

Anonymous. 1990. Interview by author. Boise, Idaho. 14 June.

Anonymous. 1990. Interview by author. San Sebastian, Spain. 10 July.

Anonymous. 1993. Interview by author. Reno, Nevada. 11 June.

Ansotegui, Dorothy Inchausti. 1993. Interview by author. Boise, Idaho, 23 June.

———. 1993. Letter to author. 23 September.

Arbeloa, Irene Orriaga. 1984. Interview by Mateo Osa and Gretchen Osa. Tape recording. Reno, Nevada. 15 May.

———. 1993. Letter to author. 23 September.

———. 1993. Interview by author. Reno, Nevada. June.

Argoitia, Virginia. 1993. Interview by author. Tape Recorded. Sparks, Nevada. 8 June.

Arrieta, M. I., B. Martinex, B. Criado, N. Labato, and C. M. Lostao. 1992. "Genetic and Dermatographic Distances among Basque Valleys." *Human Biology* 64.5: 714.

Arrizabala, Luis, and Linda Barinaga, eds. 1990. *Jaialdi '90 Program Book*. Boise: Fairview Printers.

Artiach, Miren Rementeria. 1990. "A Symposium on Basque Language and Culture: Past Perspectives and Future Prospects." Address. Boise State University. 14 June.

———. 1991. Telephone conversation with author. 12 October.

Aulestia, Gorka. n. d. "The Nationalism of Sabino de Arana y Goiri." Unpublished Essay.

———. 1978. "Mikel Zapata: Cautious Creator of Unified Basque." Unpublished Essay.

Bard, Rachel. 1982. *Navarra, the Durable Kingdom*. Reno: University of Nevada Press.

Barrutia, Victoria. 1993. Interview by author. Boise, Idaho. 23 June.

Bengochea, Concepcion. 1986. Personal History Manuscript. Glasgow, Montana.

Bengochea, Denise. 1990. Interview by author. San Sebastian, Basque Country. June.

Bieter, Pat. n.d. *The Basques of Idaho*. Boise: Idaho State Historical Society.

Bilbao, Elizabeth Eiguren, and Mary Lou Murelaga Guerricabeitia, eds. 1987. *Umearen Marrazkaik eta Amestiak*. Boise: Aircraft Press.

Boyd, William c. 1969. "Genetics and the Human Race." *Science* 140: 1057–64.

Brandes, S. 1990. "Giants and Bigheads: Metaphors of Masculinity." In *Readings for Basque Anthropology*, ed. Teresa del Valle. San Sebastian: Universidad Pais Basco: 17–36.

Brick, Joan. 1992. "A Dancing People." *The Basque Studies Program Newsletter*. April: 7–10.

Burke, Kenneth. 1954. *Permanence and Change*. Los Altos, California: Hermes.

Cavalli-Sforza, L. L., W. F. Piazza, and P. Menozzi. 1993. *History and Geography of Human Genes*. Princeton: Princeton University Press.

Cendagorta, Mary. 1993. Interview by author. Tape recorded. Reno, Nevada. 11 June.

Chisholm, Elise. 1993. Interview by author. Elko, Nevada. 4 July.

Chisholm, Jean Etcheverry Landa. 1991. Telephone interview by author. 12 February.

Clamp, Christine. 1986. "Managing Cooperation at Mondragon," Ph.D. diss., Boston College.

Clark, Robert P. 1979. *The Basques: The Franco Years and Beyond*. Reno: University of Nevada Press.

Clifford, James, and George F. Marcus. 1986. *Writing Culture: The Poetics and Politics of Ethnography*. Berkeley: University of California Press.

Collins, Roger. 1986, 1990. *The Basques*. Oxford and Cambridge: Basil Blackwell, Inc.

Coon, Carlton. 1939. *The Races of Europe*. New York: Macmillan.

Corcostegui, Lisa Tipton. 1993. Interview with author. Tape recorded. Reno, Nevada. 15 June.

————. 1994. Letter to author. 10 April.

Curutchet, Jean Louis. 1993. Conversation with author. 13 June.

Danielson, Larry. 1977. "Introduction." *Western Folklore* 36: 1–5.

Davis, Fred. 1979. *Yearning for Yesterday: A Sociology of Nostalgia*. New York: Free Press.

Decroos, Jean Francis. 1983. *The Long Journey*. Reno: University of Nevada Press.

Dégh, Linda. 1995. *Narratives in Society: A Performer-Centered Study of Narration*. Helsinki: Suomalinen Tiedeakatemia Academia Scientarium Fennica.

del Valle, Teresa. 1990. "Women's Power in Basque culture: Practice and Ideology." In *Readings on Basque and Iberian Culture*, ed. Teresa del Valle. San Sebastian: Universidad del Pais Vasco.

————. 1990. Lecture. Basque Culture Studies. San Sebastian. 9 July.

————. 1990. Lecture. Basque Culture Studies. San Sebastian, Spain. 11 July.

————. 1990. Lecture. Basque Culture Studies. San Sebastian, Spain. 17 July.

————. 1990. Lecture. Basque Culture Studies. San Sebastian, Spain. 23 July.

————. 1990. Lecture. Basque Culture Studies. San Sebastian, Spain. 1 August.

Dolby-Stahl, Sandra. 1989. *Literary Folkloristics and the Personal Narrative*. Bloomington and Indianapolis: Indiana University Press.

Douglass, William A. 1969. *Death in Murelaga: Funerary Ritual in A Spanish Basque Village*. Seattle: University of Washington Press.

————. 1976. "Serving Girls and Sheepherders: Emigration and Continuity in a Spanish Basque Village." In *The Changing Faces of Rural Spain*, eds. Joseph B. Aceves and William A. Douglass. New York: Schenkman Publishing Company.

————. 1980. "Inventing a Basque Identity: the First Basque Festival." *Halcyon 1980: A Journal in the Humanities*. Reno: Nevada.

————. 1993, 1996. Address. "Basque Identity: Past Perspectives and Future Prospects." San Francisco, 9 October. Published in *Change in the American West, Exploring the Human Dimension*, ed. Stephen Tchudi. Reno: University of Nevada Press.

Douglass, William A., and Jon Bilbao. 1975. *Amerikanuak: Basques in the New World*. Reno: University of Nevada Press.

Dredge, Alicia Aldana. 1989. Interview by author. Tape Recorded. Soda Springs, Idaho. 12 October.

————. 1989. Interview by author. Tape recorded. Soda Springs, Idaho. 23 October.

————. 1989. Interview by author. Tape recorded. Soda Springs, Idaho. 28 October.

————. 1991. Telephone interview by author. 12 February.

Duarte, Cassie. 1993. Interview by author. Tape recorded. Reno, Nevada. 11 June.

Dundes, Alan. 1989. *Folklore Matters*. Knoxville: The University of Tennessee Press.

Echegaray, Lucy Arrien. 1993. Interview by author. Elko, Nevada. 17 June.

Echeverria, Jerònima. 1988. *California-Ko Ostatuak: A History of California's Basque Hotels*. Ph.D. Dissertation. North Texas State University, May.

————. 1989. "California's Basque Hotels and their *Hoteleros*." In *Essays in Basque Social Anthropology and History*, ed. William A. Douglass. Reno: University of Nevada Press.

————. 1991. "Women's Work, Basque Style." Essay on file at the Basque Museum and Cultural Center. Boise, Idaho.

————. 1994. "Editor's Note." *Journal of the Society of Basque Studies in America*. 14: ii.

Eiguren, Joe V. 1972. *The Basque History: Past and Present*. Boise: Offset Printer.

Elorza, Benedicta. 1993. Interview by author. Tape-recorded. Reno, Nevada. 11 June

Etcheverry, Dominique. 1995. Interview by author. Rupert, Idaho. 10 April.

Etcheverry, Henry. 1990. Interview by author. Lava Hot Springs, Idaho. 15 November.

Etcheverry, Kathy. 1994. Letter to author. 17 February.

————. 1995. Interview by author. Rupert, Idaho. 10 April.

Etcheverry, Louise Savala. 1989. Interview by author. Tape recorded. Lava Hot Springs, Idaho. 8 October.

————. 1991. Telephone interview by author. 12 February.

————. 1993. Interview by author. Tape Recorded. Rupert, Idaho. 9 November.

————. 1993. Telephone interview by author. 4 December.

————. 1997. Telephone interview by author. 6 April.

Etcheverry, Nichole. 1995. Interview by author. Rupert, Idaho. 10 April.

Farmer, Alicia. 1993. Interview by author. Tape recorded. Boise, Idaho. 22 June.

Frank, Roslyn M. 1977. "The Religious Role of Women in the Basque Culture." In *Anglo-American Contributions to Basque Studies: Essays in Honor of Jon Bilbao*, eds. William A. Douglass, Richard W. Etulain, and William H. Jacobsen, Jr. Desert Research Institute Publications on the Social Sciences 13: 1553–60.

Gallop, Rodney. 1930, 1970. *A Book of the Basques*. Reno: University of Nevada Press.

Garetea, Juan. 1989. Telephone interview with author. 15 November.

Garatea, Paquita. 1990. "The Basques-Euzkaldunak." In *Jaialdi '90 Program Book*, eds. Luis Arrizabala and Linda Barinaga. Boise: Fairview Printers.

Ghiglieri, Lucille Orriaga. 1984. Interview by Mateo Osa and Gretchen Osa. Tape recorded. Reno, Nevada. 15 May.

———. 1993. Correspondence with author. 24 August.

———. 1984 Irene Orriaga Arbeloa, and Janet Inda. Interview by Mzateo Osa and Gretchen Osa. Tape recorded. Reno, Nevada. 15 May. Used with permission of the Basque Studies Library of the University of Nevada, Reno.

Goldaraz, Resu Goldaraz. 1989. Interview by author. Tape recorded. Soda Springs, Idaho. 12 November.

Goodenough, Maribelen "Mary" Goldaraz. 1991. Interview by author. Tape recorded. Soda Springs, Idaho. 12 November.

Halbwachs, Maurice. 1950. *The Collective Memory*. New York: Harper & Row.

Hauser, Maria Rosa (pseudonym by request). 1993. Interview by author. Tape recorded. Sacramento, California. 16 June.

Henningsen, Gustav. 1980. *The Witches' Advocate: Basque Witchcraft and the Spanish Inquisition (1609–1614)*. Reno, Nevada: University of Nevada Press.

Hilton, Lynn M. 1987. *Spain: Its People and Culture*. Lincolnwood: National Textbook Company.

Hobsbawm, Eric, and Terence Ranger. 1983. *The Invention of Tradition*. Cambridge: Cambridge University Press.

Hormaechea, Juanita "Jay" Uberuaga. 1993. Interview by author. Boise, Idaho. 22 June.

Ibarra, Martina. 1993. Interview by author. Tape recorded. Boise, Idaho. 22 June.

Inda, Denise. 1993. Interview by author. Tape recorded. Reno, Nevada. 14 June.

Inda, Janet Carrica. 1993. Interview by author. Tape recorded. Reno, Nevada. 14 June.

———. 1993. Telephone interview by author. 6 December.

———. 1995. Telephone interview by author. 1 April.

Inda, Mary Louise. 1993. Interview by author. Tape recorded. Reno, Nevada. 10 June.

Jausoro, Isabel. 1993. Interview by author. Tape recorded. Boise, Idaho. 22 June.

Jouglard, Cecelia A. A. 1989. Interview by author. Tape recorded. Rupert, Idaho. 16 November.

———. 1989. Interview by author. Rupert, Idaho. Tape recorded. 18 November.

———. 1990. Interview by author. Rupert, Idaho. Tape recorded. 20 March.

———. 1990. Interview by author. Rupert, Idaho. Tape recorded. 15 June.

———. 1991. Telephone interview with author. 12 February.

———. 1993. Conversation with author. Boise, Idaho. 22 June.

Kirshenblatt-Gimblett, Barbara. 1986. "Studying Immigrant and Ethnic Folklore." In *Handbook of American Folklore,* ed. Richard M. Dorson. Bloomington: Indiana University Press.

———. 1995. "Taking Stock." *Journal of American Folklore* 110: 123–139.

Landa, Bernard. 1993. Telephone interview by author. 20 November.

Landa, Christine. 1993. Interview by author. Elko, Nevada. 4 July.

Larrondo, Brad. 1993. *Euzkaldunak: Basques in Boise.* Video. May.

Laxalt, Robert. 1972. *In a Hundred Graves.* Reno: University of Nevada Press.

———. 1989. *The Basque Hotel.* Reno and Las Vegas: University of Nevada Press.

Levi-Strauss, Claude. 1966. *The Savage Mind.* Chicago: University of Chicago Press.

Malinowski, Bronislaw. 1979. "The Role of Magic in Religion." In *Reader in Comparative Religion: An Anthropological Approach,* eds. William A. Lessa and Evon Z. Vogt. 4th ed. New York: Harper Collins, 1979.

Moe, John. 1977. "Folk Festivals and Community Consciousness: Categories of the Festival Genre." *Folklore Forum* 10.2: 33–40.

Monroe, Sarah Baker. 1995. "Basque Celebrations in Eastern Oregon and Boise." In *Idaho Folklife: Homesteads to Headstones*, ed. Louie W. Attebery. Salt Lake City: University of Utah Press.

Morrison, Roy. 1991. *We Build the Road As We Travel: A Cooperative Social System*. Philadelphia: New Society Publishers.

Oring, Elliot. 1986. *Folk Groups and Folklore Genres*. Logan: Utah State University Press.

Ortiz Oses, A., and E. Borneman and R. K. Mayer. n.d. *Antropoloia vasca: simbolos, mitos y arquetipos*. Trans. Teresa del Valle. In *Readings on Basque and Iberian Culture*, ed. Teresa del Valle. San Sebastian: Universidad del Pais Basco, 1990.

Osa, Gretchen. 1989. "The Overland: The Last Basque Hotel." In *Essays in Basque Social Anthropology and History*, ed. William A. Douglass. Reno: University of Nevada Press.

Ott, Sandra. 1981, 1993. *The Circle of the Mountains*. Reno: University of Nevada Press.

Pagoaga, Julie Gogenola. 1993. Interview by author. Shoshone, Idaho. 21 June.

―――. 1993. Telephone conversation with author. 9 November.

The Post-Register. Idaho Falls, Idaho. 12 October 1989, B-7.

Robbins, Elene Aldana. 1990. Interview by author. Boise, Idaho. 14 June.

Rose, Lucille Borda. 1993. Interview by author. Tape recorded. Reno, Nevada. 30 June.

Sevilla, Maria José. 1990. *Life and Food in the Basque Country*. New York: New Amsterdam Books.

Stern, Stephen. 1977. "Ethnic Folklore and the Folklore of Ethnicity." *Western Folklore* 36.1 (January): 7–31.

Stern, Stephen, and John Allan Cicala. 1991. *Creative Ethnicity: Symbols and Strategies of Contemporary Ethnic Life*. Logan: Utah State University Press.

Swanson, Marie Borda. 1993. Interview by author. Tape recorded. Reno, Nevada. 30 June.

Thomas, Hugh. 1986. *The Spanish Civil War*. Middlesex, England: Penguin Books, Ltd.

Times-News (Twin Falls, Idaho.) 1991. "Basque Culture is Unique." 1 April: A5.

Toelken, Barre. 1996. *The Dynamics of Folklore: Revised and Expanded Edition*. Logan: Utah State University Press.

Tyler, Stephen A. 1986. "Post-Modern Ethnography: From Document of the Occult to Occult Document." In *Writing Culture: the Poetics and Politics of Ethnography*, eds. James Clifford and George E. Marcus. Berkeley: University of California Press.

United States. 1988. Department of Education. The Commission on Minority Participation in Education and American Life. *One Third of a Nation*. Washington Government Publishing Office.

———. 1990. Department of Commerce. Bureau of the Census. Ethnic and Hispanic Branch. Washington Government Publishing Office.

Urza, Carmelo. 1993. Conversation with author. Reno, Nevada. June.

Urza, Monique Laxalt. 1993. Interview with author. Reno, Nevada. 15 June.

———. 1993. *The Deep Blue Memory*. Reno: University of Nevada Press.

Wasil, Rita. 1970. "Spanish Basque Folklore." University of Oregon Folklore Archives. Eugene, Oregon.

White, Linda. 1990. Lecture. Second Session of "A Symposium on Basque Language and Culture: Past Perspectives and Future Prospects." Boise, 14 June.

Index